CW01065185

Kabbalah

Kabbalah

A Neurocognitive Approach to
Mystical Experiences

SHAHAR ARZY AND MOSHE IDEL

Yale UNIVERSITY PRESS
New Haven and London

Yale University Press books may be purchased in quantity for educational, business,
or promotional use. For information, please e-mail sales.press@yale.edu (U.S. office)
or sales@yaleup.co.uk (U.K. office).

Set in Minion type by IDS Infotech, Ltd.
Printed in the United States of America.

Library of Congress Cataloging-in-Publication Data

Arzy, S. (Shahar), author.
Kabbalah : a neurocognitive approach to mystical experiences / Shahar Arzy,
Moshe Idel. — 1st edition.
pages cm
Includes bibliographical references and index.
ISBN 978-0-300-15236-4 (hardback)
1. Cabala—Psychology. 2. Cognitive neuroscience. 3. Mysticism—Judaism—
Psychological aspects. I. Idel, Moshe, 1947– author. II. Title.
BM526.A79 2015
296.7'12—dc23
2014042891

A catalogue record for this book is available from the British Library.

This paper meets the requirements of ANSI/NISO Z39.48–1992
(Permanence of Paper).

10 9 8 7 6 5 4 3 2 1

Contents

Foreword

Steven C. Schachter, M.D.

Chief Academic Officer, Consortia for Improving Medicine
with Innovation and Technology; Professor of Neurology,
Harvard Medical School

The clues to answering age-old questions may turn out
to be just as old as the questions themselves.

In this thought-provoking book, Shahar Arzy and Moshe
Idel present compelling evidence that over hundreds of years,
a group of mystics, collectively part of the Jewish Kabbalah,
mastered techniques to probe and potentially unlock the secrets
of human consciousness, mind and body, sense of self, and
ecstatic experiences.

The substantial body of knowledge given to us by Kabbalah mystics and explored in this book complements and
greatly expands upon insights to these phenomena from other
sources. For instance, as the authors note, similar experiences
have been spontaneously reported by people in the context of
their epileptic seizures. The so-called ecstatic seizure became

widely known through the books of Fyodor Dostoevsky. In describing his own seizures, Dostoevsky said: "I experience such happiness as is impossible under ordinary conditions, and of which other people can have no notion. I feel complete harmony in myself and in the world and this feeling is so strong and sweet that for several seconds of such bliss one would give 10 years of one's life, indeed perhaps one's whole life" (as noted in *Dostoevsky: His Life and Art*, by Avrahm Yarmolinsky). Likewise, blissful states have been described in detail by non-Kabbalah practitioners of meditation.

With this immeasurably valuable treasure trove uncovered by the authors, will we, as they suggest, come closer to understanding these longstanding and beguiling issues? Can we indeed "decode the brain mechanisms and processes" by studying the mystics' methods and experiences through the lenses of modern neurological and cognitive sciences and our own worldviews?

Perhaps so, though in keeping with Kabbalah teaching, it will require patience and diligence.

Introduction

The human body and self play a prominent role in mysticism.[1] Various mystics have endeavored to achieve altered bodily states, such as a feeling of their body expanding beyond its physical limits, a feeling of "forgetting" their body, or sensing "something" filling it.[2] Some have reported perceiving the self as doubled, elevated, or semipermeable, whereas others have reported a sense of unity between self and object, a splitting of the self, or an experience of themselves in nonhabitual positions.[3] These altered states further enabled the mystics to investigate the boundaries of mind, consciousness, and self, for it is from these altered states that these obscure mental functions might be newly enlightened. In particular, practitioners of ecstatic mysticism developed complicated techniques of mental imagery, transformation, and concentration for bringing about altered conscious states; through such techniques mystics could frame their ideas and wonderments in kinds of settings that could help lead to conclusions about their own selves, consciousness, and minds.

Self, consciousness, and mind recently have become
main subjects for investigation in the nascent field of cognitive neuroscience. Dealing mostly with functions such as
memory, learning, perception, and attention, the cognitive
neurosciences started to enlarge their scope to ask questions
not only about specific functions but also about the system
that these functions serve—that is, the human self. Studies of
patients serve as a main route in these explorations. In particular, patients with altered perceptions of their bodies gave
rise to the field of bodily consciousness, and patients in dissociative states—in which the unity or continuity of consciousness, identity, and body representation are disrupted—
teach us about the importance of this integration to our
mental life.

In this book we investigate the phenomenology, neurology, and underlying cognitive mechanisms of ecstatic mystical
experiences as described in the writings of mystics of major
trends in Jewish Kabbalah, including the prophetic Kabbalah,
the Lurianic Kabbalah, Sabbateanism, and Hasidism. These
mystics achieved their most prominent mystical experiences by
using practical ecstatic techniques that changed their perceptions of body and self. We detail experiences, techniques, reports, and instructions as described by the mystics themselves.
These are compared with similar phenomena found nowadays
in neurological patients as well as investigated and induced in
healthy individuals in the laboratory. Using neurological and
neuropsychological studies, analyses of brain lesions, experimental psychology, neurophysiology, and neuroimaging, we
endeavor to decode the neurocognitive mechanisms and processes underlying these mystical experiences. This enables
further understanding not only of the mystical techniques but
also of the ecstatic experiences and their various contexts.

Several attempts have been made in recent years to explore the links between mystical experiences in various cultures and the neurosciences. Here we focus on (1) ecstatic Jewish mystics and (2) autoscopic and dissociative experiences. Readers interested in broader studies of religious experience and the brain may want to consult more general works, such as Patrick McNamara's *The Neuroscience of Religious Experience*.

The first chapter presents the main approaches to mystical experiences in religious studies and discusses the advantages and disadvantages of our phenomenological technique-oriented and brain-based approach. The second chapter highlights the central role of ecstasy in mysticism and presents the four main Kabbalistic ecstatic experiences: autoscopic ecstasy, ascension ecstasy, unitive ecstasy, and dissociative ecstasy. The third chapter analyzes autoscopic, ascension, and unitive ecstasies, differentiating them with respect to both phenomenological characteristics and underlying neurocognitive mechanisms. The fourth chapter analyzes the dissociative experience, distinguishing between trance and possession dissociation and characterizing their neurocognitive correlates. For readers not well acquainted with neurology and cognitive brain sciences, Appendix A presents information processing in the brain, discussing the main functional cerebral networks and specialized high-order brain activities relevant to this book. For readers outside of religious studies, Appendix B provides information about the main mystical figure in this book— Abraham Abulafia.

Notably, this book does not attempt to reduce the mystical experience into a "simple" neurocognitive pattern. Rather, by strict phenomenological and technical analyses, compared with modern findings of cognitive neuroscience, we try to decipher the complexity of the mystical experience by pointing to its underlying neurocognitive mechanisms. It is from these very basic elements that further investigations—such as the comparison of different mystical circles or reconstructions of rituals, techniques, and teachings—may be obtained. Moreover, we suggest that these mystics may partially share common interests of modern cognitive neuroscientists in the quest for better understanding of mind, consciousness, and self. We therefore hope that these analyses will deepen our understanding of the subjective experience that these Kabbalah mystics attempted to induce and explore. Such an approach may also favorably benefit consciousness studies and the neurocognitive understanding of the "self." As philosopher Thomas Metzinger claims, "Our traditional, folk-phenomenological concept of a 'soul' may have its origins in accurate and truthful first-person reports about the experiential content of a specific neurophenomenological state-class."[4] In other words, our contemporary reflections of consciousness, self, and mind might have emerged from the older notion of "soul" or "proto-concept of mind," which in turn may be a derivate of the introspective experiences that led humans to start reflecting about self, consciousness, and mind. The ecstatic Kabbalah mystics may therefore be considered pioneering investigators of the human self, consciousness, and mind.

I

Justification of a Neurocognitive Approach to Mystical Experiences

1. Four Main Approaches to Mystical Experiences

Important as they are for mystical and religious figures as well as for scholars of mysticism, mystical experiences are hardly accessible to investigation. A major problem is that reports, oral and written, are unable to express these most intimate and private experiences of human mental life. Moreover, most of those documents consist of terminologies, theologies, and sometimes forms of realia that differ from the mentalities and the religiosities one may encounter in ordinary life. Many religious figures, however, will eventually claim differently that tradition is so powerful that it may preserve and facilitate the repetition of the paradigmatic experiences of the ancients, even millennia after the experience. In fact, repeating these paradigms, or at least following them, might shed new light on the intimate experiences reported by the mystics.

Four main approaches attempt to understand mystical experiences. The older and the most dominant is the theological approach.[1] According to this approach, the reports and practices of the mystics allow the learning of something about the nature of the entity revealing itself in that experience: God or angels, sometimes of the demonic world. It is less the message itself than the source of the message that counts. For those who seek some form of knowledge about the nature of the deity from fathoming the accounts of revelations, the message is the representation of the otherwise hidden nature of the Supreme Being. Such a process might be seen with respect to the central book of the Jewish religion: the Hebrew Bible. Very much a mythological and not a theological book, the Hebrew Bible became the foundation of an infinite number of speculations about God and the divine world that constitutes much of Western theology. This theologization of the Bible is a matter not only of biblical studies, but also of the way in which the modern study of Jewish mysticism operates.[2] The theological approach, however, does not necessarily reflect the internal world of the experiencer or his self-interest in the mystical activity.[3] The reader might then wonder: what causes the mystic to dedicate so much effort and energy to the preparations and praxis required to attain mystical experiences instead of deriving them from authorized sources such as the Bible?

A second, more scholarly approach is concerned with the social role of the mystic as reflecting the society in which he is active rather than regarding the content of the revelation as a message directed to the society. According to this sociological approach, the mystical message might represent the "spirit" of the society in language, ethics, or practice. Thus, mystical experiences become a form of transformation of collective values into a somehow novel message that both reflects and shapes the society in which the recipient of the revelation operates. Religious documents therefore become anthropological, sociological, and historical documents that purport to represent something about a society and the interactions between that society and the elite individuals who produce the religious documents.[4] Categorically speaking, this approach does not examine the intimate world of the mystic or his self-motivation.

The third approach is psychoanalytical. Psychologists of the psychoanalytical perspective basically see the religious experience as a form of inner experience, shaped by the individual history of the person who undergoes that experience. These psychoanalysts might be able to highlight internal or psychic aspects of the mystical experience, yet they inspect religious documents dealing with such experiences mainly to elicit from those texts some general knowledge about human mental life. This might be why psychoanalysts such as Sigmund Freud and Carl G. Jung wrote so much about religious texts: they were looking for the hidden mental mechanisms as reflected in myths and symbols that expressed ancient experiences but also left their imprint on the present. To reiterate, in these cases it is not the nature of the Supreme Being or of society that stands at the center of the investigation but some form of decoding the texts in order to penetrate the unconscious, the archetype, the underlying myths probably encoded in the mystics' reports of their experiences. Yet these are related to humans in general and not to the self-interest of the mystics themselves.

A fourth approach that tried to deal with the mystical experience itself was introduced by the American psychologist and philosopher William James. In his *Varieties of Religious Experience* James analyzed as a primary source the reports of religious figures (prominent ones as well as laypeople), rather than doctrines and theories, in order to better understand usually difficult-to-investigate faculties of the human mind. In his monograph, James distinguishes between "the religion of healthy mindedness," which is associated with positive feelings and internal "harmony," and the experiences of "the sick soul," which are associated with negative physical and mental feelings. As valuable as this book is in pioneering an investigation of individual first-person reports, nevertheless a general psychopathological classification dominates it rather than the quest for understanding the mystical experience as processed in the mystic's own mind.

The four main approaches to mystical experience described here regard the texts as mirrors for a diversity of processes that inform those texts and are otherwise impenetrable. The details of the reports are conceived as important, however, not for their content but as faithful mirrors, rather than as literary documents whose strategies, genres, symbols, and linguistic layers shape the message as much as the emotional and cognitive contents that may be reflected by them. However, experiences, when investigated in documents, are not only reported but also inevitably distorted by the complexity or the ineffability of the experience, postexperiential additions, or the linguistic and literary nets that constitute the religious documents. As in many other mental and cognitive cases, language not only conveys the content of the experience, a pure vessel, but also intervenes in its articulation, either by informing it with new, extraneous concepts or by expressing the nebulous data of the experience in terms dominant in a certain environment or culture. Just as the mystical experiences are informed by a variety of preexperiential elements, so postexperiential factors, such as other terminologies and conceptual structures of thought, may also inform the reports of these experiences.[5]

Therefore, an approach that seeks theological or social content in the report might be distorted by these external factors. A more precise approach might look for the basic elements in the description that are as free as possible from linguistic and other more extrinsic factors.

2. A "Bottom-Up" Approach to Mystical Experiences

In lieu of the "top-down" form of scholarly discourse that starts with the general aspects (theology, society, archetypes, or psychopathology) as the most crucial issues for the most intimate experience that is supposed to happen to a human being, we propose here to start with the experiences themselves and what mystics do in order to attain these experiences. Instead of deciding upon the nature of a certain unitive experience according to its theoretical-general starting point, we suggest here an emphasis upon the more experiential components of the mystical event and the mechanisms in which they are processed in the mystic's brain and mind. To reiterate, instead of emphasizing the nature of the object of the mystical union as part of a theological or other general top-down discourse, we direct our attention to the expressions related to the experience itself—namely, to the mystical techniques of its attainment, to the claims of efficacy, and to its underlying cognitive, psychological, and neurophysiological mechanisms.[6] With the shift of focus from an overemphasis on the object of the experience to the experience itself, the investigation and comprehension of mystical experience may decisively change. Instead of dealing with external factors in order to establish the content of a certain phrase, we shall seek expressions related to the induction of the experience and its cognitive and neurophysiological effects, or, explicitly, we shall expose neurocognitive mechanisms that allow mystics to enter into these experiences. Indeed, such a shift also accepts descriptions of experiences whose mystical object may not be the ultimate divinity but the mystic's self or body nonetheless. Moreover, it is this "bottom-up" approach that allows a significant and valid generalization, in view of the similarity between traditions, and in some aspects even identity, of the very subject of the experience: the human brain. According to such a phenomenological brain-based approach of mystical expressions,[7] it will be less important if the Christian mystic describes his or her union with Christ or with the Father, if the Sufi relates his or her experience to the Hidr and not to Allah, if a Jewish mystic intends to become one with a lower Sefirah or even with the Agent Intellect and not with the Infinite.[8] The quality and intensity of the experience as described by the mystic may become crucial for the nature of the experience even more than the theological status of its content.[9] This assessment does not mean that general factors are of no importance, but that by definition they cannot dictate all the major aspects of the mystical experience per se.

3. Experiences, Radiations, and Cognitive Techniques

The proposed bottom-up neurocognitive approach may even allow elaborating more about the experience's radiation, which is the effect of the notions related to the mystical experience on the religious structure. Each of the major religions includes several different structures that may incorporate mystical components. These, in turn, might have a crucial effect on later developments of a certain religion, which therefore could not be understood solely by its own consequential theologies.

However, by turning the attention of the study of mysticism to the role of the mystical technique and its cognitive effects on the mystic, further crucial questions might arise: What drove the mystic to devote himself to their induction? How did the experience reward the mystic's efforts? Or did concepts—such as mystical union—significantly interact with other main cognitive concepts and practices, qualifying and being qualified by such interactions? We thus propose to look for such mutual radiations between key notions of certain mystical traditions. Such an approach will also enable us to better answer whether the occurrence of certain mystical formulae is merely a matter of convention, of sharing an en vogue vocabulary in a certain tradition without any experiential substratum, or whether it may reflect a deeper experience, by sharing mystical paths and techniques[10] and therefore similar neurocognitive processes.

Indeed, even the abovementioned general top-down approaches to mystical experiences may profit from the understanding of the radiations, core techniques, and neurocognitive processes underlying those experiences. So, for example, identifying the neurocognitive mechanisms responsible for a central mystical concept such as mystical union might be related to other mechanisms that lead to another main kind of activity, such as fulfillment of the commandments. Moreover, the introduction of mystical union as a prerequisite for the mystical intention during the performance of certain commandments with theurgical intention and for obtaining their desired influence bears evidence for a new composition of mystical techniques and might lead toward a full-fledged mystical phenomenon. Or, to take a different example: the probability that a certain unitive phrase stands for more than a repetition of a cliché but may reflect an actual experience is greater if the same mystic stresses that this phrase is derived from his own

subjective experience with techniques such as mental concentration and solitude or seclusion, equanimity, and letter combination.[11] It seems inadequate, therefore, to decide the place
and role of the mystical phenomenon in a certain literature
only on the basis of the recurrence of extreme mystical expressions; it is possible to somehow come closer to the actual
significance of extreme mystical expressions not only by examining the simple semantics of the phrase, but also by decoding
techniques used by the mystic or the group to which he belongs.
Examining these techniques and their influence on brain processes might foster a better understanding of the expression of
these techniques in the mystic's experiences and reports.[12]

Furthermore, applying a general classification to outstanding individuals, like the prominent mystics, might reduce or at
least deviate our understanding of their unique self-interests.
With respect to theology, for example, some of the more learned
among the mystics were presumably acquainted with more than
one theology—some quite different from each other. The following example may illuminate the question: Abraham Abulafia, a thirteenth-century ecstatic mystic, was well acquainted,
in addition to biblical and rabbinic material, with Maimonides'
Neoaristotelian theology, with the synthesis between the an-
thropomorphic and more speculative theology of the early-
thirteenth-century Hasidei Ashkenaz, with sefirotic theosophies
of Catalan Kabbalists, and with Arabic and scholastic philoso-
phies (for more on Abulafia, see Appendix B). He apparently
studied some of these before his first mystical experiences, and
the expressions of his experiences take into consideration a
variety of elements from some of these diverse forms of thought.
His experiences therefore are not unified or characterized by
one underlying theological or philosophical approach; rather,
they are affected by the rich and complicated techniques he

used and their influence on certain brain mechanisms, as we shall see. Though Abulafia may be considered a rather extreme case, the same is true, though to a lesser degree, in many other cases in the multilayered Jewish culture, as Judaism developed as a minority religion in a variety of cultural environments: more than one theology was known, acceptable, or at least available to the mystics. An approach that would emphasize a spiritual discipline as essentially dependent on the experience's technical triggers and the triggered neurocognitive mechanisms could integrate the different sources into a relatively coherent framework.

4. Technical Constructivism from Within the Brain: Limitations

Although the top-down theological, social, archetypical, or psychopathological types of constructivism can be problematic, the bottom-up approach might provoke the danger of technical constructivism. By this latter term we point to the effect of the techniques' details on the structure of the theology. Nevertheless, there is a certain substantial difference between the two forms of constructivism: while the top-down forms are prone to being exclusive and inhibiting, technical constructivism can be envisioned as inclusive. A variety of experiences can be induced by the same mystical technique—given the diversity of the spiritual physiognomies of the mystics as well as environmental influences—and in some cases a variety of techniques are available within the same mystical system. Moreover, although it is possible to postulate a certain affinity between the nature of the techniques and the content of the experience induced thereby, these techniques can incite unexpected experiences.[13] In addition, the conservative top-down approaches perceive the mystic as a representative of a certain religion or society and at the same time perceive the nature of the experience as a derivate of this religion or society, thus determining a closed loop. However, if we assume a significant affinity between the mystical experiences, the mystical techniques, and the underlying neurocognitive mechanisms, we may speak about a form of relationship that is much more open-ended; we may then attempt to offer forms of categorization that will account for the types of mystical techniques and their effect on the brain. Such a proposal has its strength, perhaps, but also its limitations, and it is worthwhile to emphasize the latter.

One limitation is that the forms of mystical experiences that may be correlated to a certain type of theology are much more numerous than those that may be related to specific mystical techniques, as a scholar may be quite hesitant in reconstructing a mystical technique without solid evidence but will, at the same time, more easily venture to create an affinity between a mystical experience and a theological stand. Second, not all mystical experiences are related to mystical techniques.[14] This relative absence is more evident in the Christian-Western forms of mysticism than in the Christian-Orthodox ones or in Hindu, Japanese, or Muslim forms of mysticism. Phenomenologically speaking, however, Jewish mysticism belongs more to the latter group than to the former despite most of its main developments occurring in the Latin West.[15] The relation between theology in general and mysticism in particular and the neurosciences has attracted much attention in recent years in scholarly literature, religious communities, and the general public. With the flourishing of neuroimaging techniques, many neuroscientists have recorded the brain activity of mystics during their practices in order to decode the "neural mechanism" underlying these practices. However, merely the "brain mapping" of brain activations correlated with certain practices has a very limited value. Here, we endeavor to use neurological, neuropsychological, and neuroimaging data as a platform for supplying an explanatory value to the mystical materials.[16]

The interplay between the concepts and practices conceived as being mystical determinants is the nature of mystical literature. Yet this interplay relates to the way the concepts represent the mystical experience itself rather than to the religious or social systems. In our case, with respect to the centrality of the notion of mystical union in Jewish mysticism, for example, the experience itself is more important than the attempt to define it in a certain way, namely, that it stands for union or communion. Top-down approaches can develop an interesting typology of the meanings of mystical union but at the same time ignore its meaning to the mystic himself as expressed in his most intimate experience. It is the affinity between the mystical technique, as used by the mystic, and the altered neurocognitive system that may clarify the nature of the mystical union in a certain circle differently from one in which the mystical techniques are different. More impressive, in our opinion, than reading the Upanishads, Yogi treatises, the exercises of St. Ignatius, or Sufi mystical treatises is the existence of mystical techniques that are supposed to induce deep mystical transformations that further lead to these fascinating theologies. Likewise, it seems that the specific regula of a certain Christian order may bear evidence of its mystical character much more than the general theology shared by all Christian orders. It is in the *principium individuationis* that better clues for the understanding of the specifics of mystical experiences should be searched.

We therefore propose that it is more reasonable to deduce the mystical nature of a system from its practices and their cognitive characteristics than to reduce mysticism to a "spiritual" potentiality related to a certain theological belief or to abstract ideas such as theism, pantheism, or panentheism.[17] Instead of working from the top down—that is, starting with the theological stand and deriving the kind of mysticism—we propose to adopt the bottom-up approach, starting with the details of the mystical practices and then advancing toward the experiences molded by these practices.[18]

Moreover, we propose to begin the technical constructivism from the most basic and common foundation of the mystical experience: the human brain. Assuming that beyond theological, social, archetypical, or psychopathological differences all mystics share similar neurocognitive mechanisms, we hypothesize that similar techniques will influence the cognitive system in a similar manner. Thus, decoding these basic mechanisms might supply us with a basis for reconstructing the experience of the mystic and his group. This reconstruction might further allow comparison of different mystical groups, nets, schools, or trends and the detection of their mutual influence. Crucial for the understanding of the differences or similarities between Jewish mysticism and any other form of mysticism will be not the very existence of the mystical experiences or expressions, but the more comprehensive neurocognitive mechanisms within which they eventually function. By investigating the various kinds of mystical paths and techniques—constructing them on the basis of the underlying neurocognitive mechanisms and then correlating them with the mystical ideals—one might more reasonably decide whether a certain ideal was cultivated in fact rather than consisting in a theoretical goal. The detailed description and analysis of the mystical path, the question of the occurrence of initiation rites, the intensity of the mystical techniques, and the underlying cognitive processes and brain mechanisms may together testify to the extreme nature of experiences more than to the kind of theology that governs a certain religion. In this book we emphasize this route from technique through cognition to the brain and then to the ecstatic forms of the mystical experience. But before discussing the techniques themselves, we introduce ecstatic mystical experiences.

II

Approaching Ecstatic Experiences

1. Ecstasy and the Subjective Experience

Experiences are not given events, and even less so objects. They are basically remembered inner events, sometimes remembered after lengthy periods of time. Furthermore, they are oftentimes formulated in terms reflecting terminologies or worldviews that mystics adopted after the experience occurred. If ecstatic experiences are involved, the awareness of what happens during these events is even less plausible. To stand outside oneself ("out-of-body"), which is the meaning of "ecstasy" (*ex-stasis*), and to feel what is going on inside is a conundrum that challenges a most intimate and straightforward human state. Moreover, it requires the alteration of neurocognitive mechanisms that normally act otherwise—namely, to unify self and body. Thus, as elusive and volatile as mystical experiences are, ecstatic experiences are even more imponderable, and their literary expression is more indebted to conventions and terminologies that constitute forms of adaptations of the inchoate cognitive and psychological events in the form of transmittable narratives. When interrogating the meaning of ecstasy, it does not suffice to analyze the semantics of the word by resorting to dictionaries and encyclopedias; we should also carefully examine the ways in which various mystics have used the term with respect to their own subjective experiences. Here we suggest a neurocognitive approach from within the brain that might supply a framework for understanding the ecstatic experiences through the underlying neurocognitive mechanisms rather than through terminologies or semantics. Before delving into this cognitive and neural basis, we should first define ecstatic experiences.

We can identify several major meanings of ecstasy in the modern scholarship of mysticism. There is no agreement, however, upon a major type of experience as ecstatic. Interestingly, it was Martin Buber at the beginning of the twentieth century who wrote about the ancient meaning of ecstasy similarly to our proposal: "Ecstasy is originally an entering into God, *enthusiasmos*, being filled with the god. Forms of this notion are the eating of the god; inhalation of the divine fire-breath; loving union with the god (this basic form remained characteristic of all the later forms of mysticism); being reborn through the god; ascent of the soul to the god, into the god."[1] The richness of the "notion" of ecstasy encompasses most forms of mysticism. Remarkably, Buber himself preferred a view of ecstasy that is related to the unity of the self experienced by the mystic during his ecstatic experience. Unlike the manner in which Buber describes the original meaning, replete with references to God, his own understanding is much more individual and anthropocentric, in line with the proposed neurocognitive approach. This shift from the general to the individual represents a major change in modern scholarship.

Scholars studying ecstasy have attempted to adopt one basic feature of the many features attributed to ecstasy in Buber's passage, applying it to certain techniques and experiences. So, for example, Mircea Eliade, whose book *Shamanism* has the subtitle "Archaic Techniques of Ecstasy," takes ecstasy to be a state of consciousness during which the shaman ascends to other worlds.[2] Following this track is one of the most erudite and innovative books on ecstasies—Ioan P. Couliano's monograph titled *Expériences de l'extase*—a book that has unfortunately remained at the margins of scholarship on the topic, both in general studies and in Judaica. In this book the term "ecstasy" basically stands for the journey of the soul through various supernal realms, heavens, or planets in some Greek, Hellenistic, and Jewish literature of late antiquity. Looking at the titles of Couliano's other books, the English revision of his earlier book titled *Psychanodia I: A Survey of the Evidence Concerning the Ascension of the Soul and Its Relevance* and his later book *Out of This World: Otherworldly Journeys from Gilgamesh to Albert Einstein*, we can well perceive his main intention when resorting to the term "ecstasy": it involves out-of-body experiences, basically a celestial journey. Though the material under scrutiny in Eliade and Couliano is disparate—Asian Shamanism in the former and Hellenistic and Jewish material in the latter—the meaning of the term "ecstasy" in each is rather similar: challenging the habitual self of embodiment, ex-stasis per se manifested as out-of-body experiences and/or the ascent of the soul to other realms for various aims. The author of another earlier book on ecstasy, Ioan M. Lewis, in his *Ecstatic Religion: An Anthropological Study of Spirit Possession and Shamanism*, also interprets ecstasy as "dis-embodiment," and the phenomena of possession represent the thrust of his analyses. Though the material Lewis uses is closer to Eliade's than Couliano's, his emphasis differs from that of Eliade, who did not conceive the phenomenon of possession as an essential feature of Shamanism.[3]

More comprehensive is the resort to the term "ecstasy" in the more recent monograph of Jess B. Hollenback, who sees in the term "ex-stasis" out-of-body experiences that include a variety of modes, such as journeys of the soul (out of the body) and autoscopy (seeing an image of oneself outside the physical body), though not the category of trance and possession: "Ecstasy often appears in mystical literature to refer to an intense state of exaltation, bliss, and thrilling excitement that is often of such intensity that the mystic loses awareness of both his or her physical environment and body. . . . Ecstasy also has a second connotation that implies an even more radical process of abstraction from the body and the physical world."[4]

Following these thinkers, we propose integrating these various meanings of ecstasy. To reiterate, we propose seeing ecstatic experiences as including out-of-body experiences, autoscopy, and trance/possession. The expressions that may be described as states of ecstasy recur especially in the literature of ecstatic Kabbalah, which, under the influence of Abraham Abulafia's thought, developed at the end of the thirteenth and beginning of the fourteenth centuries. However, this is actually part of a wider structure, the ecstatic model, which includes practices discussed in this book. Thus, various elements of the ecstatic model are easily detectable in Neoplatonic philosophy and in Geronese Kabbalah. The gist of the description below has to do with covering a variety of experiences in which the self is imagined to be, in one way or another, in (embodied) or out of (disembodied) the body, or replaced by another "personality" in the physical body. In order to enable an investigation of these experiences, we shall first check the existence of the different categories of embodiment in Jewish material and attempt to avoid referring to the more diffuse and vague meaning of ecstasy as a feeling of elation, intoxication, excitement, or rapture that is sometimes found in scholarship and in some mystical texts.[5]

2. Ecstasy in Judaism

Attempting to describe Judaism is challenging. It is not only a matter of the polymorphous nature of the phenomenon, as we shall see immediately, but also that Judaism is an ongoing process, whose recent articulations project backward into the past and depend on our understanding of that past. Even more difficult is to describe ecstasy in Judaism. With the exception of Philo of Alexandria (an important one), the Greek term "ex-stasis" was never—as far as we know—used by a Jewish mystic or even by a traditional Jew before the twentieth century. The problem is to identify Hebrew terms or descriptions that may correspond to ecstasy or to experiences related to what has been conceived of as ecstatic in the senses mentioned above. We shall deal here with three major concepts of ecstasy: disembodiment (the divestment of corporeality), prophecy, and alterations of consciousness. The exact meaning of these concepts is not yet clear (and not yet comparable to terms for ecstasy in other traditions, such as *wajd* or *wujud* in Islam, or Hindu views related to Tantra, or parallels in Shamanism). In Jewish mysticism, however, all the categories mentioned above may be found and, notably, be related to certain techniques.[6] In this we differ from the opinion of the most prominent scholar of Kabbalah, Gershom Scholem, which is worth noting.

When describing the earliest extensive brand of Jewish mystical literature, the Heikhalot literature of late antiquity,

Scholem emphasizes that "ecstasy there was, and this fundamental experience must have been a source of religious inspiration, but we find no trace of a mystical union between the soul
and God. Throughout there remained an almost exaggerated
consciousness of God's otherness, nor does the identity and
individuality of the mystic become blurred even at the height
of ecstatic passion."[7]

This emphasis on the difference between ecstasy and *unio-
mystica* (mystical union) recurs in Scholem's description of all
the major forms of Jewish mysticism. "No trace of mystical
union" is a strong negation. Later on in the same book he
further states:

> It is only in extremely rare cases that ecstasy signi-
> fies actual union with God in which the human in-
> dividuality abandons itself to the rapture of the
> complete submission in the divine stream. Even in
> his ecstatic frame of mind the Jewish mystic almost
> invariably retains a sense of the distance between
> the Creator and His creature . . . he does not regard
> it [ecstasy] as constituting anything so extravagant
> as identity between the Creator and creature.[8]

It is interesting that Scholem distinguishes, at least implicitly,
between moderate ecstasy and extreme forms that may culminate in union. Scholem's emphasis on the basic difference between Creator and creature recurs in his vision of Judaism.
In fact, the predominance of this ontological distance, which
Scholem attributes to the classic Kabbalistic text the *Zohar* is
the explanation he proposes for its extraordinary success.[9] Indeed, Scholem restricts the extreme forms of ecstasy exclusively to Abraham Abulafia's Kabbalah but claims that even in

the writings of Abulafia's followers "there is little of the latter's ecstatic extravagance, and ecstasy itself is moderated into *devekut* [unio-mystica]." Nevertheless, he admits that in the school of the leading Hasidic master of the mid-eighteenth century, Rabbi Dov Baer of Mezeritch, descriptions of "ecstatic abandon" exist.[10]

To summarize Scholem's view of ecstasy: he occasionally admits that ecstatic experiences are found in three major forms of Jewish literature: the Heikhalot literature of late antiquity, Abulafia's medieval Kabbalah, and premodern Polish Hasidism. He sometimes also described the messianic figure of Sabbatai Zevi (1626–ca. 1676) as an ecstatic. Even in those cases, however, Scholem attempts to relegate the extreme forms of ecstasy to the margin of his general picture of Jewish mysticism. The attempts that Scholem's students made to qualify his stronger demarcation between Jewish mysticism and other forms of mysticism having descriptions of unitive experiences even further reduced the realm of ecstatic experiences in Jewish mysticism. This stands against our claim that (1) ecstasy is a major form of mysticism, including Jewish mysticism; and (2) ecstasy plays a major role in developing a bottom-up approach to the study of mystical experiences.

In fact, Scholem's view of ecstasy represents a later version of a strong and widespread phenomenology of religion, found in an influential distinction that became a tradition in the scholarship of religion and is therefore worth mentioning here. So, for example, in his classic book on ancient Judaism Max Weber wrote:

> The prophet never knew himself emancipated
> from suffering, be it only from the bondage of sin.
> There was no room for a *unio-mystica*, not to men-

tion the inner oceanic tranquility of the Buddhistic *arhat*. . . . Likewise his personal majesty as a ruler precluded all thought of mystic communion with God as a quality of man's relation to him. No true *Yahwe* prophet and no creature at all could even have dared to claim anything of the sort, much less the deification of self. . . . The prophet could never arrive at a permanent inner peace with God. *Yahwe*'s nature precluded it. There is no reason to assume the apathetic-mystic states of Indian stamp have not also been experienced on Palestinian soil.[11]

A sharp distinction is drawn between the divine and human beings, even the prophet. In ancient Judaism, according to Weber, "there was no room for a *unio mystica*," and the prophet or the mystic "could [not] even have dared to claim anything of the sort." The awareness of this distinction and the ensuing suffering are described as characteristic of the ancient Jewish or biblical religious landscape, a fact that precludes the blurring of the gap between God and humanity. Moreover, the nature of God hinders a more peaceful relationship between him and his emissary, the prophet. An immanent struggle is postulated, which shapes the nature of the experience. The sharp distinction between the prophetic and the mystical has been inherited from Weber and also used by Friedrich Heiler in his famous book on prayer and by Arnold Toynbee in his stark phenomenological juxtaposition of the Judaic and the Buddhaic families of religion.[12] In this vein, Robert Zaehner also wrote as follows:

If mysticism is the key to religion, then we may as well exclude the Jews entirely from our inquiry: for

Jewish mysticism, as Professor Scholem has so ad-
mirably portrayed it, except when influenced by
Neo-Platonism and Sufism, would not appear to be
mysticism at all. Visionary experience is not mystical experience: for mysticism means if it means
anything, the realization of a union or a unity with
or in something that is enormously, if not infinite-
ly, greater than the empirical self. With the *Yahweh*
of the Old Testament, no such union is possible.
Pre-Christian Judaism is not only un-mystical, it is
anti-mystical, as is the main stream of Protestant-
ism—and for the same reason: each is exclusively
obsessed by the transcendental holiness of God
and man's nothingness in the face of Him. The Jews
rejected the Incarnation and, with it, the promise
that as co-heirs of the God-Man they too might be
transformed into the divine-likeness; and it is
therefore in the very nature of the case that Jewish
"mysticism" should at most aspire to communion
with God, never to union.[13]

In many of his writings Zaehner is trapped in his stark theological distinction between theistic mysticism, positive in his
opinion, and the monistic, which he disregarded. However, even
in the case of a theistic religion like Judaism, real or genuine
experiences are prevented by another stark theological assump-
tion: only the belief in incarnation ensures genuine mystical
experiences. It seems that this erudite scholar of mysticism was
not acquainted with Philo and possible contributions of his
views on mysticism and ecstasy and on nascent Christian mysticism. It seems that Philo even influenced Plotinus's vision of
mystical union.[14] Western mysticism has, therefore, not only

a phenomenology, but also a history, and Philo preceded all the Neoplatonists' and even the Middle Platonists' discussions of ecstasy and mystical union. In any event, here there seems to be some agreement between the most prominent scholar of Jewish mysticism and other major scholars of mysticism regarding the limited forms of ecstasy—a view that ensures maintaining the difference between Judaism and other forms of religion in matters of mysticism.

On the other hand, in Western Europe there was a certain reticence toward the concept of ecstasy. As we can see in the survey of Hywel David Lewis, and in the much earlier description of ecstasy by Roger Bastide, it has oftentimes been regarded with suspicion. Sometimes "good" ecstasy, namely Christian ecstasy, was juxtaposed to the negative, almost "suicidal" ecstasy of the Hindus.[15] In fact, some of the "negative" categories in the study of religion, such as magic, regarded with suspicion by the Inquisition or church authorities, return slowly in the nomenclature of scholars. Ecstasy should be understood, together with magic or enthusiasm, as a category that has been more recently, and partially, emancipated from the negative halo of earlier generations of thinkers and scholars. Just as the Enlightenment and the traditional forms of Christianity contributed to suppressing some uneasy aspects of religion, also in Judaism the effect of Jewish rationalism, as represented by Maimonides and later figures of the Jewish Enlightenment, contributed to the suppression of the role played by magic, myth, enthusiasm, and ecstasy.[16] So, for example, one of the major analyses of the concept of prophecy in the Bible, Abraham J. Heschel's *The Prophets*, written originally in Berlin in the 1930s, sharply distinguishes between prophecy and ecstasy, assuming that prophets were not ecstatics. Some of the main Jewish figures who studied in Berlin, and were contemporaries of Heschel, were quite reticent to admit the existence of ecstatic experiences in Judaism, as is the case of R. Joseph Baer Soloveitchik and Yeshayahu Leibowitz. In the last generation, however, the affinity between prophecy and ecstasy has been strongly emphasized. Moreover, the affinity between the two concepts is found explicitly in some medieval views of prophecy (e.g., *Quis Rerum Divinarum Heres Sit*, nos. 68–70, 259–265) and even before that in Philo of Alexandria, as we have seen.[17]

Even Buber's *Ecstatic Confessions*, a groundbreaking collection of texts in its time, allowed ecstasy quite a modest place in Judaism. The timid admissions of the existence of ecstatic experiences in mystical forms of Judaism seem like understatements in the light of what happened in the last generation of earlier rabbinic scholarship. A prominent example supporting our approach is the mode of prayer, described as ecstatic prayer, cultivated by two main Mishnaic figures, Rabbi Hanina ben Dossa and Rabbi Akiva. Phenomenologically speaking, their prayer constituted an invasion of the divine within the person praying, who was aware of the efficacy of the prayer by its smoothness.[18] Ecstasy is thus not confined to particular small groups in Judaism but is also represented in founding documents of Rabbinism—the Mishnah and the Talmud.

Moreover, as recently demonstrated, ecstatic experiences, including unitive ones, can be found in Jewish mysticism to a much greater degree than Scholem and his followers claimed.[19] The ecstatic element in Jewish mysticism should thus be understood as an important constant of a varying intensity rather than the prerogative of a certain phase or school. However, the nature of ecstasy in Jewish mysticism as expressed in its phenomenological, technical, and philosophical characteristics has not yet been tackled in a systematic manner. A preliminary attempt to begin to do so is made here.

3. Four Basic Levels of Ecstasy in Jewish Mysticism

Generally, we should distinguish among four basic levels of ecstasy:

1. The ecstatic description: various descriptions of ecstatic experiences, reported by the mystic.
2. The ecstatic model: namely, the conjugation between a technique and an experience ensuing from resorting to the technique.
3. Ecstatic Kabbalah: a school that produced a literature that gravitates around the centrality of attaining an ecstatic experience.
4. The ecstatic brain: neurocognitive mechanisms that are altered by the ecstatic technique, giving rise to the ecstatic experience.

The descriptions of an ecstatic experience (level 1) may appear in a variety of literatures, such as poetry or autobiography, or even in Kabbalistic books that have other religious foci as their main concern. The ecstatic model (level 2) is much more restricted and is found in Kabbalistic forms of literature or their sources (level 3), via alterations of certain neurocognitive mechanisms (level 4), though those cannot discriminately characterize a certain school. The ecstatic model (level 2) can be conjugated to other Kabbalistic models and may be related to more complex structures (level 4).[20] Ecstatic Kabbalah (level 3) is a school that not only deals with techniques and descriptions of experiences, but sees them as the focal point of religious life. It therefore includes both the descriptions of the experience and the ecstatic model, or models, but attributes to them a centrality that differs from the mere recording of the ecstatic experience. Consequently, ecstatic Kabbalah creates a new religiosity much more focused around the ultimate role of the ecstatic experience, and it therefore also imparts a special role to altered consciousness. A description of an experience and a discussion of an ecstatic model may move from an ecstatic Kabbalist to another who does not belong to this school without transforming the new literary milieu into a treatise belonging to ecstatic Kabbalah. Furthermore, Kabbalistic trends that traditionally belong to a circle not considered an ecstatic type of Kabbalah, such as Lurianic Kabbalah, might demonstrate characteristics and writings with a highly ecstatic emphasis. A deep look into the descriptions, models, and techniques that different mystics use might therefore lead to a remapping of ecstasy in Jewish mysticism.

4. Four Types of Ecstatic Experience in Jewish Mysticism

Following the descriptions above, we may distinguish among four major subtypes in ecstatic Kabbalah: autoscopic ecstasy, in which the mystic has the impression of seeing an image of himself in the extracorporeal space; ascensional ecstasy, in which the mystic experiences leaving the body, paralyzed or asleep, with a paranormal experience of encountering "heavenly entities"; unitive ecstasy, which is the experience of unification with the divine; and dissociative (possessive) ecstasy, in which an "external entity" inhabits the mystic's mental state. These four forms of ecstasy hold a triple process in common: first, general intention toward a separation of the "soul" from the body, reflected in the prefix "ex-" in the term "ecstasy" (ex-stasis); second, the occurrence of a unique ecstatic event, which differs from one category to another; and third, each of those experiences being related to a distinct neurocognitive mechanism. After the moment of "mental dissociation," the mystic experiences an alteration of his habitual experience of himself as residing in the physical body, although this feeling differs from one category of ecstasy to another.[21]

Traditionally, this process embraces two phases. The first is mutative (*mutatis mutandis*), related to what is known as *via purgativa* (the way of purification) and to techniques to remove common experiences in order to prepare for the higher experiences, approximating *via unitiva*. The occurrence of the second phase involves a change in the mystic's habitual subjective experience of the location of the self, from residing within the physical body (embodied) to a new altered experience (embodied or disembodied). This alteration of the habitual sense of self differentiates ecstatic experiences from more general unitive experiences in which expressions of a nonhabitual sense of self are not essential. A distinct change in self- and body-processing is characteristic of the four main types of ecstatic experiences we survey in this book and is parallel to the way in which each experience differs from one Jewish mystical school to another.

To reiterate, unlike most mystical phenomena, which are described as unitive or communitive, ecstasy involves a moment of dramatic shift or change in the experience of the self because the ecstatic techniques aim to challenge the mystic's habitual experience of body and self. It is therefore not just the intensification of earlier forms of activity, or the mental imagery of the mystic's self to what he assumes is a higher entity, though these processes may be part of the path followed by ecstatics. Ecstasy is thus less a continuous development that may culminate in arriving at or adhering to a divine source than it is a sudden event, which may indeed be expected, cultivated, and induced. This induction is performed through the use of certain techniques that in turn operate on specific neurocognitive mechanisms that challenge the mystic's habitual perception of the self.

5. Ecstasy and the Cognitive Neuroscience of the Self

Recently, a new domain joined the relatively new field of cognitive neuroscience: the study of the human self. Scientists have now begun to refer not only to "perception" or "action," but also to the "perceiver" or "actor," that is, the human self. Similarly to mystical experience, the nascent study of the self has a special interest in phenomena in which self and body are dissociated. Not only within the field of cognitive neurosciences, the study of the human self has also developed in parallel in philosophy and psychology.[22] A main source of evidence in the study of the self is clinical observations from neurology and psychiatry, including conditions in which the habitual perception of self and body is challenged. These conditions include, for instance, asomatognosia (the feeling that part of the body does not exist or is out of corporeal awareness), delusional misidentification syndromes (belief that a person, object, place, or event is duplicated or replaced), and phantom limb (the vivid impression that an amputated limb is still present).[23] Recent evidence demonstrates that these phenomena are not only found in pathological states of the human brain, but are also inducible in healthy subjects by various manipulations or focal electrical cortical stimulation. This accords with observations of some of these experiences being found in the healthy population.[24]

Recently, cognitive neuroscience began to define and explore different processes that are related to the self and might be disturbed in various clinical conditions and laboratory settings. These include phenomena such as agency (the sense of being the one who is causing or generating an action) and ownership (the sense of being the one who is undergoing an experience), which are disturbed in dissociative states. These processes also include the distinction between self and other, as challenged in delusional misidentification syndromes, as well as visuo-spatial perspective taking and spatial unity between self and body, which are disturbed in autoscopic phenomena.[25]

In fact, these faculties are the cognitive processes that are disrupted during ecstatic experiences. In contrast to religious studies, however, cognitive neurosciences can get behind the phenomenological reports and further explore them by using various methods, such as clinical evaluation, neuropsychological examination, anatomical and functional neuroimaging, electrophysiological recording, induction by a variety of manipulations or in virtual reality, and various experimental paradigms in both healthy subjects and neurological and psychiatric patients. Here we apply this approach in order to explore ancient mystical reports. We gather evidence from experimental psychology, phenomenology, clinical neurology, and functional brain imaging in order to further understand how different techniques that mystics used influenced neuro-cognitive processes and how these processes further led to their reported mystical experiences. Notably, this is not an attempt to demystify these experiences (as demystification does not serve hermeneutics)[26] or to simply reduce the mystical experience to a neurocognitive pattern. Rather, by a strict analysis of the phenomenological reports and the techniques used, in comparison to modern findings of cognitive neuroscience using the abovementioned methods, we try to decipher the complexity of the mystical experiences by decoding their underlying cognitive mechanisms. These might be later reconstructed for mystical experiences as practiced or formulated by different mystical schools, circles, and trends. Such an analysis, we hope, will deepen our understanding of the subjective experience that these outstanding mystical figures endeavored so intensely to evoke in their own selves.

III

The One out There
Autoscopic Phenomena in Jewish Mysticism

1. Ex-Stasis: Out of the Body

Ecstatic mystics from various traditions and periods used altered bodily states in order to develop concepts of mind and consciousness.[1] This is reflected in the term "ex-stasis," which might be understood literally as "out-of-body experience." In particular, certain ecstatic Jewish mystical schools, many of them led by prominent Kabbalistic figures, devoted their efforts to developing and practicing cognitive techniques aimed at inducing out-of-body and related experiences in order to extend concepts of mind, embodiment, and the mental world.[2] Out-of-body experiences belong to a group of experiences known as "autoscopic phenomena," defined as illusory visual experiences during which humans have the impression of seeing an image of their own body in an extrapersonal space.[3] As for mystical experiences, the importance of these phenomena to the study of the "self" is derived from the isolation during these experiences of a fundamental component of the self as one experiences oneself beyond one's habitual corporeal boundaries. In this kind of experience, one may see oneself from a different perspective and might consequently achieve novel insights about the nature of the self. This, in turn, may supply the experiencer with novel observations that may be of importance for both cognitive and mystical points of view.

This chapter discusses different kinds of ecstatic Kabbalah experiences in relation to the modern investigation of autoscopic phenomena. Various groups from ecstatic Kabbalah that voluntarily induced ecstatic experiences by using specific techniques are described and their detailed reports are compared with the experiences of contemporary healthy people and those of patients with brain damage in order to understand the cognitive mechanisms behind the phenomena.[4] The comprehension of ecstatic experiences with respect to known neurological phenomena, as autoscopic phenomena indeed are, may facilitate further understanding of religious and mystical experiences. As we have said, instead of exploring these complex phenomena from the top down, according to their historical backgrounds or theosophical meanings, here we investigate them from the bottom up, from the basic phenomenological and cognitive characteristics behind the experience as well as their underlying brain mechanisms, the generators of their induction.[5] We begin with a survey of autoscopic phenomena as classified by modern cognitive neuroscience.

2. Autoscopic Phenomena

Three distinct forms of autoscopic phenomena have been defined (Figure 1):[6]

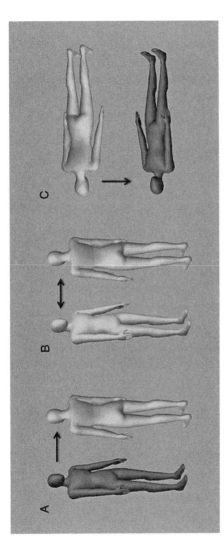

Figure 1. Autoscopic phenomena. A: *Autoscopy* is the experience of seeing one's body in extracorporeal space (as a "double"). The self is experienced as localized inside the boundaries of the physical body. The double (right) is seen from the habitual egocentric visuo-spatial perspective (left). B: *Heautoscopy* is when one see one's body and the world in an alternating or simultaneous fashion from both extracorporeal and bodily visuo-spatial perspectives. C: During an *out-of-body experience* one appears to "see" oneself (bottom figure) and the world from a location above the physical body (extracorporeal location and visuo-spatial perspective; top figure). The self is localized outside its physical body (disembodiment) (adapted from M. Peer, R. Lyon, and S. Arzy, "Orientation and disorientation: lessons from patients with epilepsy." *Epilepsy Behav* 41 [2014]: 149–57; with permission).

1. *Autoscopy:* During autoscopy, people experience their "self" or center of awareness within the physical body, seeing a "double" of themselves in extrapersonal space viewed from the perspective of their own physical body. People who experience autoscopy usually describe how the impression of seeing an image of themselves in front of their eyes resembles looking into a mirror or seeing a picture of themselves. The autoscopic image is localized centrally, approximately one meter from the experiencer's physical body. The experience is usually mostly visual and is mainly experienced when the person is in a sitting or standing position.

2. *Out-of-body experience:* One is awake and feels the center of awareness as located outside the physical body and somewhat elevated. From this location one experiences seeing one's body and the world, resulting in perceptions organized consistently with this visuo-spatial perspective. This experience combines three phenomenological elements: the feeling of being outside the body (disembodiment), a change in the visuo-spatial perspective, and seeing one's own body (autoscopy). The following example from Harvey Irwin (a psychologist interested in the psychological bases of the "paranormal") may illustrate people's experience during an out-of-body experience: "I was in bed and about to fall asleep when I had the distinct impression that 'I' was at the ceiling level looking down at my body in the bed. I was very startled and frightened; immediately [afterward] I felt that I was consciously back in the bed again."[7]

3. *Heautoscopy:* This is an intermediate phenomenon between autoscopy and out-of-body experience. During heautoscopy, people also see their "double" in extrapersonal space; however, it is difficult for them to decide whether they are "disembodied," that is, whether their sense of self is localized in the physical body or in the autoscopic body. Therefore, people experiencing heautoscopy may see the world from two simultaneous or alternating visuo-spatial perspectives: the habitual physical visuo-spatial perspective and the extracorporeal perspective. For instance, a neurological patient experiencing heautoscopy described that when he got up from bed, he turned around and saw himself still lying in the bed. He was angry about "this guy who I knew was myself and who would not get up and thus risked being late at work." He tried to wake up the body in the bed by shouting at it, then by shaking it, and then by repeatedly jumping on it. His double did not show any reaction. Only then did the patient realize that he should be puzzled about his double and became increasingly scared by not knowing which of the two bodies he really was (or where his self was located). This was especially so because he experienced his self-location to be alternating between the two bodies. His only intention was described as trying to become one person again.[8]

Autoscopic phenomena are mainly described visually (as reflected by their name). However, they are not a purely visual experience and thus do not originate in visual disturbance. Autoscopic phenomena have several associated nonvisual sensations, including vestibular sensations (such as floating, elevation, lightness, tilting, or vertigo); body schema disturbances; and visual body part illusions (such as the shortening, transformation, or movement of an extremity).

Although autoscopic phenomena are most often related to clinical situations, they have been found to occur in 10 percent of the general population, perhaps once or twice in a lifetime.[9] Likewise, autoscopic phenomena in the healthy population have been illustrated in many cultures and expressed in art, literature, ceremonies, and myths. Self-portraits have been common in art from time immemorial, but some prominent modern Western artists have been fascinated by autoscopic phenomena. Pablo Picasso drew abstract and colorful doubles; Frida Kahlo was engaged by her suffering body and self, expressing it by various autoscopic positions (interestingly, she used a mirror attached to the ceiling of her bed for her self-portraits); René Magritte also challenged the possible perspectives of autoscopic phenomena. In literature, authors such as Fyodor Dostoevsky, Guy de Maupassant, and Orhan Pamuk wrote about doubles, and Jorge Luis Borges elaborated on "Borges and I." Autoscopic phenomena also have been used in mystical and magical traditions from ancient times. One of the texts of Hellenistic magic, the "Mithras Liturgy," contains a passage that speaks of man's "perfected body." Gnostic literature also portrays meetings between man and a primal celestial image, the *Doppelgänger*. According to the Hymn of the Pearl, also called the Hymn of the Soul, from the Acts of Thomas, this meeting is one of the highest forms of self-knowledge, comparable to Eastern methods of yoga, Iranian Zoroastrianism, and oriental-Greek Hesychasm.[10]

Comparably, autoscopic phenomena have played a key role in the most influential trends of Jewish mysticism, which have in turn influenced central Christian and Muslim movements.[11] Various ecstatic Kabbalistic circles managed to induce different types of autoscopic phenomena. Three of these will be presented below with descriptions of experiences and approaches to inducing such phenomena. This will be followed by a detailed phenomenological analysis and discussion of the similarities and differences of the experiences with respect to contemporary autoscopic phenomena in healthy subjects and neurological patients. We shall then try to decode the neurocognitive mechanisms stimulated by the various techniques and finally evaluate the contribution of such an analysis to understanding these mystical experiences and their influence on Jewish mysticism.

3. Autoscopic Phenomena in Ecstatic Kabbalah

In parallel to the three major forms of autoscopic phenomena, we may distinguish among three major forms of experiences in ecstatic Kabbalah: autoscopic ecstasy, ascension ecstasy, and unitive ecstasy. These forms have a double process in common: first is an impression of seeing a second body in the extrapersonal space, reflected in the prefix "ex-" in the term "ex-stasis." Then a mentally associated event occurs, altering the mystic consciousness and differing from one category to another (like feelings of ascension or unification to/with the divine). Moreover, all three experiences are related to specific techniques devoted to removing the common habitual embodied experience sensation in order to prepare the mystic for the ecstatic experience of a dramatic shift in corporeal awareness. In this way, ecstasy is less a continuous development that may culminate in adhering to/with a divine source than a sudden event that may be expected, cultivated, and induced. Here we review these three main ecstatic forms and underpin the techniques required to induce ecstatic experience.

AUTOSCOPIC ECSTASY

Autoscopic ecstasy is reported in the religious heritage of many traditions.[12] In the Kabbalah its main representative is Rabbi Abraham Abulafia, a thirteenth-century mystic who mainly lived in southwestern Europe (see Appendix B). His mystical method focused on the nature of the human being and ways to reach states of prophetic-like ecstasy. The method was based on specific techniques, experiences, and perceptions, unlike other, theurgic Kabbalists, who endeavored to describe the structure of the divine and the processes therein. Abulafia envisioned his prophetic-ecstatic Kabbalah as more advanced than previous forms since it dealt mainly with linguistic matters. Thus, he invented a special technique using as its basic components the twenty-two Hebrew letters and their combinations. The main "prophetic-ecstatic" experience was characterized by the visual appearance of a human form. This form had the appearance of the mystic himself (a double, or *Doppelgänger*) and talked to the mystic. This linkage of linguistics and human form is derived from the late antiquity "Book of Creation" and from the idea that a demiurgic power is hidden in the speech and the letters. Abulafia and his followers detailed their methods and induction techniques in their writings, describing their various sensations and experiences during ecstasy.[13]

The ecstatic Kabbalists referred to the feeling of an "autoscopic" body as a higher mystical achievement compared with other forms of mystical experience. In these other traditions the eventual goal is the achievement of maximal concentration by repeating a simple formula, but Abulafia suggested a method based on a stimulus that continuously changes. His intention was not to relax the consciousness through meditation (as suggested by M. Bowers and S. Glasner),[14] but to "purify" it via a high level of concentration that required the simultaneous performance of many actions. For this, he used letters. He proposed taking two "names," each containing up to seventy-two letters, and pairing them, resulting in as many as five thousand combination variations (Figure 2a). He added one of five possible vowels to each letter, creating up to twenty-five thousand combinations. This technique may be related to absorption, which is considered an important factor in autoscopic phenomena: an individual in a state of absorption has a "heightened sense of the reality of the object of attention, even when the object is imaginal."[15] To this base, Abulafia suggested adding physiological maneuvers and mental imagery, similar to those utilized in modern experiments in cognitive science that use such techniques to induce similar conditions (Figures 2b, 2c).[16]

Abulafia's method includes three steps. In the first, preparation, the mystic writes out different letter combinations (Figure 2a). In the second step, physiological maneuvers, the mystic chants the letters in conjunction with specific respiratory patterns and head positioning. In the third step, mental imagery of letters and human forms, the mystic imagines a human form and himself without a body. Then the mystic "draws" the letters mentally, projecting them onto the "screen" of the "imaginative faculty," meaning that he mentally imagines the patterns of Figure 2a. He then rotates the letters and turns them. As Abulafia describes in *Imrei Shefer:*

> And they [the letters], with their forms, are called
> the Clear Mirror, for all the forms having brightness

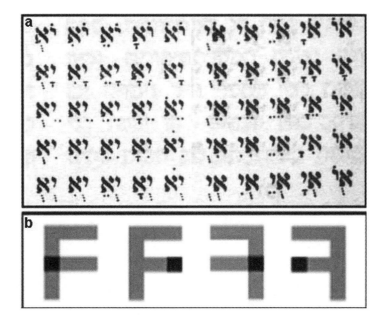

Figure 2. Cognitive tasks that alter perceptions. Figure a: Combinations of pairs of letters and vowels (א = A; י = y) before and after transformations in Abulafia's letter-combination task. The signs above and below the letters are the vowels, which indicate a different expression of each pair. Figure b: The four different stimuli as used in a modern letter-transformation task, designed to distinguish self-related (first-person perspective) mental rotation from external mental rotation (O. Blanke et al., "Linking out-of-body experience and self processing to mental own-body imagery at the temporoparietal junction." *J Neurosci* 25 [2005]: 550–57; used with permission).

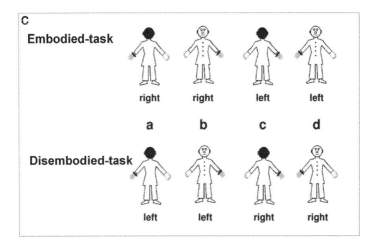

Figure c: Modern human-figure transformations task. Four different stimuli as used in the "embodied" (top) and "disembodied" (bottom) mental imagery tasks of own-body are shown (adapted from S. Arzy, G. Thut et al., "Neural basis of embodiment: distinct contributions of temporoparietal junction and extrastriate body area." *J Neurosci* 26 [2006]: 8074–81; used with permission). The stimuli are schematic human figures, facing toward or away from the participant, with either the left or right hand marked such that it appeared to be wearing a gray glove and a black ring at the wrist. Both tasks involved right-left judgments regarding whether the marked hand of the figure corresponded to the right or left hand but differed in the mental operations required to reach these judgments. In the embodied task, participants were asked to make right-left judgments after having imagined that the figure would be their reflection in a mirror; this involved visual body imagery from their own visuo-spatial perspective (embodied). In the disembodied task, participants were asked to make right-left judgments after having imagined themselves to be in the body position of the figure and as having its visuo-spatial perspective (disembodied). The correct right-left judgments per task are indicated under each stimulus.

and strong radiance are included in them. And
one who gazes at them in their forms will discover
their secrets and speak to them, and they will speak
to him. And they are like an image in which a man
sees all his forms standing in front of him, and then
he will be able to see all the general and specific
things.[17]

Notably, a core characteristic of the letter-combination technique
is absorption (a state of mental concentration), as Abulafia in-
structs the practitioner in *Sefer ha-Hesheq:* "and the one who
draws them [the letters] should think as they are speaking with
him like a man to his friend and as they are themselves men with
speech ability."[18]

We can distinguish four stages of Abulafia's autoscopic
ecstasy experience. The first is an experience of body-photism,
or illumination, in which light not only surrounds the body but
also diffuses into it, giving the impression that the body and its
organs have become light. As the ecstatic Kabbalist continues
to practice—combining letters and performing physiological
maneuvers—the second experience results: the weakening of
the body in an "absorptive" manner as described above. Subsequently, the mystic may feel an enhancement of his thoughts
and imaginative capacity. This is the third experience. The
fourth is characterized mainly by fear and trembling. Abulafia
emphasizes that trembling is a basic and necessary step in obtaining prophecy.[19] Elsewhere he writes, "all your body will
begin to tremble, and your limbs begin to shake, and you will
fear a tremendous fear . . . and the body will tremble, like the
rider who races the horse, who is glad and joyful, while the
horse trembles beneath him."[20] For Abulafia, the fear is followed
by an experience of pleasure and delight. This feeling results

from sensing another "spirit" within the body, as he describes in *Otzar Eden Ganuz:* "And you shall feel another spirit awakening within yourself and strengthening you and passing over your entire body and giving you pleasure."[21] Yet a feeling of happiness is rare in descriptions given by Abulafia's followers. As one of his students, Rabbi Nathan ben Sa'adyah Har'ar, writes (in *Sha'arei Tzedeq*): "enormous trembling seized me, and I couldn't gather strength, and my hairs stood up."[22] Only after passing through these four stages does the mystic reach his goal: the vision of a human form, which is closely linked to his own physical appearance and generally is standing in front of the mystic. The experience is increased when the autoscopic form (or double) begins to talk to the mystic, teaching him the unknown, answering his questions, and revealing the future.[23]

ASCENSION ECSTASY

The theme of "ascent to heaven" is often mentioned in spiritual biographies of religious figures: mythical figures in Mesopotamian religions, the founders of some faiths, Siberian shamans, apocalyptic figures, Greek medicine men, or Jewish *tzaddiqim* (righteous). The "heavenly journey" depicted as an act of leaving the body is found in ancient Kabbalah in the Heikhalot literature and then in Safedian Kabbalah and Hasidism, which emphasized autoscopic bodily forms of the ascent. Remarkably, these bodily forms are unique compared with the widespread traditions of ascent of disembodied "souls" in Muslim, Christian, and other mystical sources.[24] The theme of the "ascent to the divine realm" is well represented in Jewish sources of late antiquity, especially in the Heikhalot literature, written between the third and ninth centuries, which describes ascents consisting mainly of the elevation of some forms of

autoscopic body to the "supernal realm." According to Morton
Smith, "we can fairly conclude that one or more techniques for
ascent into heaven were being used in Palestine in Jesus' days,
and that Jesus himself may well have used one" and ascended,
"whether in the body or out of the body."[25] Indeed, the founders of the three major monotheistic religions—Moses, Jesus,
and Mohammed—are described as being masters of the ascent
of the soul, as they sustained their mystical experiences for long
periods. Interestingly, all three had their revelations while ascending high mountains, reporting similar corporeal experiences and hallucinations.[26] In the ninth century such techniques
were also used, as described by Rav Hai Gaon in his Responsa:
"he [the mystic] must follow a certain procedure. He must fast
a number of days and place his head between his knees and
whisper many hymns and songs whose texts are known from
tradition. Then he perceives, within himself and in the [internal]
chambers, as if he saw the seven palaces with his own eyes, and
it is as though he entered one [heavenly] palace after another
and saw what is in there."[27] The ascent of the soul gained im-
petus from sixteenth-century Safedian Kabbalah onward.
Rabbi Isaac Luria (1534–1572) is reported in hagiographic books
as one "whose soul ascended nightly to the heavens and whom
the attending angel came to accompany to the celestial academy."[28] A detailed report of the ascension technique is supplied
by Luria's main disciple, Rabbi Hayim Vital. In his booklet
Sha'arei Qedusha he mentions the technique of *hitbodedut*—
mental concentration in solitude—not present in any other
Kabbalistic source:

> Meditate in a secluded house as above, and wrap
> yourself in a *talith* [prayer shawl], and sit and close
> your eyes and remove yourself from the material

world, as if your soul had left your body, and ascended into the heavens. And after this divestment, read
one *mishna* [postbiblical literature], whatever one
you wish, many times, time after time, and intend
that your soul commune with the soul of the *tanna*
[authors of the *mishna*] mentioned in the *mishna*.[29]

Vital also emphasizes that the exit of the soul is not "as it happens in sleep," like dreaming, but upon the activity of mental
imagery: "because if it is so this is not a prophecy but a dream
like all the dreams. However, the dwelling of the Holy Spirit
upon man takes place while his soul is within him, in a state
of awakeness, and she will not exit from him." Vital was also
acquainted with what we would call today synesthetic theories
concerning the visualization of the letters of the divine name
in different colors, letters imagined to ascend on high: "he
visualized that above . . . there is a very great white curtain, upon
which the Tetragrammaton is inscribed in white as snow, in
Assyrian writing [Hebrew letters] in a certain color."[30]

Eighteenth-century Hasidism preserves a unique version
of the ascent on high. According to some texts, its founder—
Rabbi Israel ben Eliezer (Ba'al Shem Tov, or the Besht, 1698–
1760)—is reported to have performed several ascents of the
soul. Moreover, according to his eschatological theory, redemption will come when the techniques and experience of ascending on high are disseminated to many followers. The Besht's
ascension technique combines isolation (*hitbodedut*) and practices (*hanhaga*), on one hand, and a certain type of mental
imagery (*yichudim*) combined with repetitive incantation,
on the other. This is supposed to be a combination of the
Lurianic traditions mentioned above with a practice brought
from Asia to the Moldavian Carpathians by a tribe of Magyars

(Csangos). Thus, this aspect of Hasidism is a unique synthesis of primordial themes and concepts, traditions as old and primal of those of the Paleolithic Age and as late and refined as those of the Renaissance and early modern religiosity.[31]

UNITIVE ECSTASY

If mysticism is the quintessence of religion, the quintessence of mysticism is the sense of union with God. The intensification of religious life that characterizes most forms of mysticism culminates in altered experiences, whose literary expression appears in descriptions of unitive relations with supermundane beings and sometimes ultimately with God. Stemming from standard religious terminology or philosophical texts, these statements attempt to convey an experience that surpasses ordinary states of consciousness. As Plotinus put it: "The barrier between the infinite and the finite is thrown down, and the former is brought into immediate contact with the latter, so that every distinction and relation of the finite vanishes away."[32] Aristotelian terminology primarily provided concepts for what is called "intellectual union." According to Aristotelian epistemology, during the act of cognition, the knower and the known, or the intellect and the intelligible, become one. This is true for both human and divine acts of intellection. In the case of human intellection, God is the object of the intellect, and the experience amounts to what is known as mystical union. Another important source of motifs, concepts, and terms supplying significant material to Jewish medieval mysticism was Neoplatonism, which was mainly interested in the union of the soul with its roots, the universal soul, or, at times, God. Typical of Neoplatonic thought are the transformation of the particular soul into the universal soul or the ascent of the soul or its return as being central to the mystical experience.

Abraham Abulafia's explanations of the mystical experience are important in the Aristotelian trend in Jewish mysticism; he describes this experience as a cleaving or union of the human intellect to its source in the "active intellect" or even in God, the "supreme intellect." This union is the result of the epistemic act that, according to Aristotelian psychology, involves the complete identification of the intellect and its intelligibles, in this case, the "active intellect" or God.[33] Indeed, the unification with the "supreme intellect" is but a veiled reference to God. Thus, one of Abulafia's students, the anonymous author of *Sefer ha-Tzeruf*, indicates the possibility of cleaving to God: "When your intellect becomes pure, though it is still in matter, in these same [material] substratums, it indeed attains a high degree, to cleave to *causa causarum* after the separation of the soul from the matter."[34] This separation might hint at the consequence of Abulafia's technique mentioned above in which the "self" alternates with an autoscopic image. Thus, a younger member of this mystical circle, Isaac of Acre, states that the technique of letter combination might also lead to mystical unity: "I, Isaac of Acre . . . say to the elite as well as to the vulgus, that whoever wishes to know the secret of the connection to his soul to the supernal and the cleaving of his thought to the high god . . . must set before his eyes the letters of the divine name."[35]

Under Neoplatonic influence, the Italian Kabbalist Menahem Recanati, an important mystic at the turn of the thirteenth century who had a far-reaching influence on European thought, describes the technique of mystical unity, instructing the practitioner to mentally imagine a human form as engraved before him, so when linking one's "soul to the supernal soul, these things increased and expanded and revealed themselves . . . engraved in the heart."[36] The anonymous author of *Ma'arekheth ha-'Elohuth* (early fourteenth-century Catalonia) describes the position of the mystic during unitive ecstasy (which begins here with ascension on high): "The soul of the righteous one will ascend—while he is yet alive—higher and higher, to the place where the souls of the righteous [enjoy their] delight, which is 'the cleaving of the mind,' and the body will remain motionless, as it is said: 'But you that did cleave unto the Lord your God are alive every one of you this day' " (Deut 4:4).[37]

These short examples show how mystical unity is an important theme in different trends in Jewish mysticism. In the next section, we gather detailed reports by various mystics about their experiences and the techniques they used and try to classify them according to the abovementioned subtypes of ecstatic mystical experiences and autoscopic phenomena.

4. Personal Reports of Mystical Experiences

Here we present examples of each of the three ecstatic phenomena—autoscopy, heautoscopy, and out-of-body experience—as reported by prominent ecstatic mystics. Some are first-person reports, and others are expressed as instruction to a future follower or student. The similarity between the descriptive directives and the first-person reports, as well as the fact that the authors detail techniques to induce such experiences, suggests that the instructions were probably based on first-person experiences.

MYSTIC 1: ABRAHAM BEN SHMUEL ABULAFIA

Abraham Abulafia describes many times in his writings the experience of having a vision of a human "form," though initially it is not clear what this form is. As the dialogue between the mystic and the form proceeds, the reader understands that the form is the image of the mystic himself. Addressing his readers in *Sefer ha-Hesheq*, Abulafia further elaborates the scenario:

> ... and sit as though a man is standing before you and waiting for you to speak with him; and he is ready to answer you concerning whatever you may ask him, and you say "speak" and he answers ... and begin then to pronounce [the name] and recite first "the head of the head" [the first combination of letters], drawing out the breath and at great ease; and afterwards go back as if the one standing opposite you is answering you; and you yourself answer, changing your voice.[38]

Apparently, on pronouncing the letters of "the name" with specific breathing techniques, a human form should appear. Only in the last sentence does Abulafia suggest that this form is "yourself." Yet elsewhere he clarifies this explicitly, as he explains in another book, *Sefer Hayei Haolam Haba:* "And consider his reply, answering as though you yourself had answered yourself."[39]

Most of Abulafia's descriptions are written in a similar fashion. Yet in *Sefer ha-Oth*, Abulafia describes a similar episode but from an explicit self-perspective. At first, the imagined form appears to be that of another man:

I saw a man coming from the west with a great
army, the number of the warriors of his camp being twenty-two thousand men. . . . And when I saw
his face in the sight, I was astonished, and my heart
trembled within me, and I left my place and I
longed for it to call upon the name of God to help
me, but that thing evaded my spirit. And when the
man had seen my great fear and my strong awe, he
opened his mouth and he spoke, and he opened my
mouth to speak, and I answered him according to
his words, and in my words I became another
man.[40]

When one reads this passage, it becomes clear that the image is
of another man and that the mystic himself becomes "another
man" through the experience. However, further reading suggests
that "the man" is Abulafia himself because the man is "seen"
as having "a letter inscribed in blood and ink . . . like a shape
of a staff separating them, and it was a very hidden letter."
On the same page Abulafia continues that this "letter" is the
very sign of himself: "I looked [at him], and I saw there [in my
heart] my likeness and image moving in two paths": he becomes
like "another man," who is an autoscopic image of Abulafia
himself.[41]

These "two paths" in which the mystic "becomes" like the
double, and the double in turn reflects the mystic, is defined as
heautoscopy. Abulafia's reports include several components of
heautoscopy. One is a strong affinity between the mystic and
the double ("answering as though you yourself had answered
yourself"). Another is the auditory phenomenon in which the
double "opened his mouth and he spoke, and he opened my
mouth to speak." Moreover, Abulafia emphasizes the influence

of the double's speech on the autoscopic experience: "in my words I became another man"—it is through the speech that the experience happens. As exemplified in the first quotation above from *Sefer ha-Hesheq*, Abulafia describes the autoscopic experience: "go back as if the one standing opposite you is answering you; and you yourself answer, changing your voice." This is heautoscopy since Abulafia experienced his self to be localized in two positions at the same time: in his physical body and in the double's imaginary body. In addition to visualization, Abulafia also describes speaking of the "double" and an auditory dialogue between the physical and the autoscopic body in which words and thoughts are shared. Interestingly, while contemporary descriptions of heautoscopy demonstrate similar features, such as seeing an identical image that the experiencer perceives as another person, very rarely are these visual features followed by a dialogue between the experiencer and the double.[42] Finally, it is worth mentioning that Abulafia describes the double as standing and elaborates on the antecedent feelings of fear and trembling, which subsequently turn to delight.

MYSTIC 2: NATHAN BEN SA'ADYAH HAR'AR

An explicit description of autoscopic phenomena is also found in the words of Abulafia's student Nathan ben Sa'adyah Har'ar. In *Shushan Sodot*, a late-fifteenth-century book by R. Moshe of Kiev, Har'ar is quoted as saying: "Know that the perfection of the secret of prophecy for the prophet is that he should suddenly see the 'form' of himself standing before him." He states further that "one will then forget one's own self, which will then disappear from the subject. And the person will see the form of his self in front of him speaking with him and telling him the future."[43] Har'ar describes an experience of seeing a double, accompanied by depersonalization (disappearance of the experiencer's own self), followed by speech of the double. Depersonalization is a component of heautoscopy: the experiencer is dissociated from his original physical body to reside within the autoscopic body. Here again, the double is standing, as is the mystic's body. Further references can be found in Har'ar's book *Sha'arei Tzedeq*. When he began practicing Abulafia's method, he had not yet succeeded in inducing autoscopic phenomena despite his efforts: "And, with the combinations method and isolation it happened to me; what happened with the light I saw going on with me as I mentioned in *Sha'arei Tzedeq*. However, seeing a figure of myself standing before me, this I was unable to do."[44]

This description contributes to the reliability of the present phenomenology. In addition, while inducing autoscopic phenomena, Har'ar encountered various premature features, which are sometimes ignored because of the predominant emphasis on the form's appearance. As previously noted, through fasting and sleep deprivation, thought acceleration occurred, causing him to feel that his forehead was "going to be broken." He also describes absorption: "and all of these letters, one should move them in a fast movement which warms up the thought and increases eagerness and happiness."[45] And he describes physical and emotional experiences—"enormous trembling seized me, and I couldn't gather strength, and my hairs stood up on end"[46]—and the experience of body photism:

> . . . on the third night [of practicing the technique] after midnight, I nodded off a little, quill in hand and paper on my knees. Then I noticed that the candle was about to go out. I rose to put it right, as oftentimes happens to a person awake. Then I saw

that the light continued; I was greatly astonished,
as though, after close examination, I saw that it issues from myself. I said: "I do not believe it." I
walked to and fro all through the house and, behold, the light was with me; I lay on a couch and
covered myself up, and behold, the light was with
me all the while.[47]

This experience of body-photism was hypnagogic, that is, it
occurred between waking and sleeping, which has been described as a classical situation in autoscopic phenomena.[48]

Finally, regarding auditory sensations (at the time of writing *Sha'arei Tzedeq*), Har'ar was not able to hear the double.
Nevertheless, he heard a voice that emerged involuntarily from
his own throat: "Behold, like the speech which emerges from
my heart and comes to my lips, forcing them to move; and I
said that perchance, God Forbid, it is a spirit of folly which has
entered me, and I perceived it speaking [matters of] wisdom. I
said that this is certainly the spirit of wisdom."[49] This is not
speech of the double himself, as described by Abulafia, or "hearing of a presence" (hearing an invisible figure speaking),[50] since
in the latter the subject generally hears someone else speaking
behind him, whereas Har'ar heard someone speaking within
his body. A similar report is supplied by a modern neurological
patient, whose autoscopic experience occurred while climbing
at high altitude: "I heard someone speaking French. The voice
seemed to emanate from within my own body, and I heard
myself responding. It was in French too—amazing, if you consider that I do not speak French at all."[51] Therefore, this may be
a variant of the double's speech in addition to the direct speech
and the "hearing of a presence."

MYSTIC 3: ISAAC BEN JACOB HA-KOHEN

Isaac ben Jacob ha-Kohen of Soria, Spain, is another important Kabbalist. An older contemporary of Abulafia, Ha-Kohen showed great interest in autoscopy and might have influenced Abulafia's school. His mystical technique is reported by Rabbi Meir ibn-Gabbai in *Sefer 'Avodath ha-Qodesh:*

> All [the mystics] agree they possess the form of a body, similar to [that of] a human being, and very awesome. And the prophet sees all sorts of his powers becoming weaker and changing from form to form, until his powers cast off all forms and are embodied into the power of the form revealed to him, and then his strength is exchanged with the angel who speaks with him. And that form gives him strength to receive prophecy, and it is engraved in his heart as a picture . . . the prophet casts off that form and returns to his original form, and his limbs and strength come back as they were before and are strengthened, and he prophesies in human form.[52]

This is a classical description of heautoscopy: at first, the experiencer's "powers" are "embodied" in the double and then "return" into his "original form." The experience is also associated with the sensation of awe and weakness, and the double is regarded as "the angel who speaks" to the mystic, teaching us indirectly that here again we are dealing with a speaking double.

MYSTIC 4: ISAAC BEN SHMUEL OF ACRE

While practicing Abulafia's technique, Isaac of Acre reports:

... this supernal spirit of holiness suddenly comes
... only heavenly voice speaking within it, teaching
him [the mystic] sciences which have never been
heard or have never been seen. . . . [All this will hap-
pen] after he has stripped off every corporeal thing
because of the great immersion of his soul in the
divine spiritual world. This "container" will see his
own form, literally standing before him and speaking to him, as a man who speaks to his friend; and
his own [original] form will be forgotten as if his
body doesn't exist in the world . . . their soul stands
opposite them in the form of the very "container,"
speaking with them, and they say that the Holy
One, Blessed Be He, speaks with them. And what
caused them this great secret? The stripping out of
sensory things by their souls and their divestment
from them and the embodiment in the Divine
Spirit.[53]

He also adds a personal description: "one day I was sitting and
writing down a Kabbalistic secret, when suddenly I saw my body
form standing in front of me, and my self disappeared from
me, and I refrained from writing, but I was compelled."[54]
Isaac of Acre describes some fundamental characteristics of
heautoscopy: first, the experience of depersonalization ("my
self disappeared from me"; "his own form will be forgotten");
second, the visuo-spatial perspective alternating between the
physical body and the double; and third, the standing position
of the double, which is common in both autoscopy and heautoscopy. Though Isaac of Acre does not elaborate on emotions,
he was "compelled" by the experience.

MYSTIC 5: ELNATHAN BEN-MOSHE QALQISH

Elnathan ben-Moshe Qalqish, a mid-fourteenth-century Kabbalist active in the Byzantine Empire, analyzes the autoscopic phenomena evoked by Abulafia's technique and emphasizes the component of absorption. He claims that by completely concentrating on the process of letter combination, one can shut out all external stimuli. The internal thought can be "externalized," causing the illusion that one's own figure exists or speaks independently:

> . . . for every apprehension which man receives of the spiritual apprehensions, its beginning is in human thought, and when man thinks continually . . . and views all corporeal and bodily matters as the image of contingent things and spiritual matters as the essential ones . . . and he shall do all this by combining the holy letters and words and the pure language, which are the vehicles of all thoughts, then born from their combination are thoughts of wisdom and understanding, and, because of its intense meditation upon them, the intellect will perceive reality, and the renewed spirit will come . . . and will speak by itself, but the thinker will recognize that there is a mover and cause which causes him to think and to speak and to guide and to compose until, through the great [mental] activity [of the technique], the inner one will return as if externally apprehended, and the two of them, the one apprehending and the object of apprehension, are one thing, and they are mentally apprehended.[55]

Though Qalqish's is not an explicit description, by analyzing his experience, one can make some inferences about some aspects of the heautoscopical phenomenology. There is an "external" form that speaks to the mystic, the "internal." The two are one and seem to exist simultaneously, while the self seems to extend and include both forms. The experience of the external form is described as an illusion with some degree of depersonalization, while both forms are "mentally apprehended." Here again, the double speaks to the mystic "by himself," giving rise to the desired achievement of the mystic.

MYSTIC 6: YEHUDA BEN-NISSIM IBN-MALKA

Yehuda ben-Nissim ibn-Malka was probably active in northern Africa in the mid-thirteenth century. He also suggests that the induced "form" reflects the physical appearance of the mystic, as described in *Kitab Uns Utafsir:*

> I have seen with my own eyes a man who saw a power in the form of an angel while he was awake, and he [the angel] spoke with him and told him future things. The sage [angel] said: "Know that he sees nothing other than himself, for he sees himself front and back, as one who sees himself in a mirror, who sees nothing other than himself, and it appears as if it were something separate from your body, like you." In the same manner, he sees that power, which guards his body and guides his soul, and then his soul sings and rejoices, distinguishes and sees.[56]

Since this description lacks the depersonalization or association with the double of the previous descriptions, it is therefore an example of autoscopy rather than heautoscopy.

The double is described as "separated" from the body, with a weak affinity between the physical and autoscopic body. There is no hint of depersonalization or disembodiment. Interestingly, the mystic refers explicitly to mirrorlike reflections to describe the autoscopic events. This analogy has also been mentioned by patients with autoscopy (hence the older term for autoscopy—"specular hallucinations").[57] However, similarly to the previous descriptions of heautoscopy, Ibn-Malka describes a speaking double. Through autoscopy he achieved "prophecy," though he does not feel that it derives from himself as he does not have a personal association with the double. Interestingly, the experience of seeing "himself front and back" described here is quite close to mental transformation as in experimental procedures designed to investigate autoscopic phenomena in modern laboratories (discussed below).

MYSTIC 7: SEFER HA-HAYIM

The anonymous early-thirteenth-century writing *Sefer ha-Hayim*, written in France (sometimes attributed to Abraham ibn-Ezra), states that "in the manner that a man sees a form within the water or the form of the moon or the form of some other thing or the form of himself . . . he sees his own image in the light of God and His glory, and this is a form against my eyes."[58] This form appears while the mystic prepares himself for the prophetic experience. Another paragraph in the anonymous Kabbalistic text emphasizes the "specular" nature of the experience "as one looks in a mirror."[59] The experience is described as a direct derivation of the mystical technique:

> . . . a vision occurred when a man is awake and reflects upon the wonder of God, or when he does

not reflect upon them, but pronounces the
Holy Names or those of angels in order that he
be shown [whatever] he wishes or be informed of a
hidden matter, and the Holy Spirit then reveals
itself to him ... and he trembles and shakes
from the power of the holy spirit and is unable to
stand it.[60]

Though not detailed, the accounts point to autoscopy, as
suggested by the description of the "form" as a mere image
of the mystic, the "mirror" image that characterizes autoscopy,
and the absence of descriptions of depersonalization and
affinity between the autoscopic and physical body.

MYSTIC 8: HAYIM VITAL CALABRESE

Active in Safed, and then in Jerusalem and Damascus,
Hayim Vital (1543–1620) was the most important disciple of
Rabbi Isaac Luria, one of the main heroes of Safedian Kabbalah, and the inscriber of Luria's teachings. In his mystical
diary *Sefer ha-Hezionoth* (The Book of Visions), Vital reports
his experience of "ascension on high":

Once I fainted deeply for an hour, and a huge number of old men and many women came to watch
me, and the house was completely full with them,
and they all were worried for me. Afterwards the
swoon passed, and I opened my eyes and said:
"Know that just now my soul ascended to the Seat
of Glory and they sent my soul back to this world,
in order to preach before you and lead you in the
way of penance and charity."[61]

Elsewhere (in *Sha'arei Qedusha*), Vital describes the technical preparations necessary for the imagery ascent:[62]

> He should remove all his thoughts, and the imaginative power . . . will cease to imagine and think and ruminate about any matters of this world as if the soul departed from him. Then the imaginative power transforms his thought so as to imagine and conceptualize, as if he ascends to the supernal worlds to the roots of his soul that are there. . . .
> [He should] remove his thoughts from all matters of this world, as if his soul had departed from him, like a person from whom the soul departed and who feels nothing. . . . And he should imagine that his soul has departed and ascended, and he should envision the upper worlds, as though he stands in them . . . and he should concentrate in his thought.

This experience might be regarded as a variant of an out-of-body experience. First, it involves a sense of disembodiment or separation between the mystic and his body, "as if his soul departed from him." Second, the feeling of "ascension" is a common characteristic of out-of-body experiences. Third, out-of-body experiences are mostly reported while a person is in a supine position, while autoscopic hallucination and heautoscopy are mostly reported in sitting position. Fourth, the description misses an explicit autoscopic image, yet the mystic sees the scene around his physical body from above (elevated third-person perspective). In addition to the habitual out-of-body experience, Vital describes envisioning the upper world and its inhabitants, reminiscent of a "near-death experience," which often includes an out-of-body experience although here some fundamental components are missing, such as the experience of passing through a tunnel and seeing light).[63]

MYSTIC 9: ISRAEL BEN ELIEZER BA'AL SHEM TOV ("THE BESHT")

The founder of Hasidism, Israel ben Eliezer ("the Besht"), is described as someone whose "soul was ascending and the body remained as still as a mineral, and he spoke with the Messiah and with the Faithful Shepherd, and they gave answers to his questions" while "their body [of the Besht and followers] is thrown down like a stone for only a short hour or two, no more."[64] The Besht describes his alleged ascent on high as a first-person report in a letter to his brother-in-law, Rabbi Gershon of Kitov:

> On *Rosh ha-Shana* of the year 5507 (1746), I performed an incantation for the ascent of the soul, known to you. And in that vision I saw wondrous things . . . and it is impossible to describe and to tell what I saw and learned in that ascent hither, even in private. But when I returned to the lower Paradise, I saw the souls of living and dead persons, both of those with whom I was acquainted and of those with whom I was not acquainted . . . numberless, in a to-and-fro movement, ascending from one world to the other . . . and I asked my teacher and master to come with me as it is a great danger to go and ascend to the supernal worlds . . . so I ascended degree after degree, until I entered the palace of the Messiah.[65]

It is evident that this was not a unique event but a practice performed formerly by the two correspondents, using a technique
well known to them. In another paragraph the Besht reports:

> I asked the Messiah: "When are you coming?" And he
> answered: "You will know [the time] which is when
> your doctrine will be revealed in public, and it will be
> disclosed to the world and 'your fountains will well
> outside' with what I have taught you and you have
> apprehended, and also they will be able to perform
> the unifications and the ascents of the soul as you do"
> ... then [my mind] was calmed and I thought that it
> is possible for my contemporaries to attain this de-
> gree and aspect by these [practices] as I do, namely to
> be able to accomplish the ascents of souls, and they
> will be able to study and to become like me.[66]

Although the Besht is best known as the founder of Hasidism and popularized religious worship and teaching through
numerous Hasidic tales, his main interest is revealed in this rare
original and personal text to be the practice of mystical techniques aimed at inducing the experience of ascension on high.
The clear description of disembodiment and ascension reveals
this experience to include features of an out-of-body experience.
As in Vital's reports, the cataleptic-like state ("thrown down
like a stone") appears here again as well as some components
of a near-death experience. Additionally, a dialogue is described
between the mystic and the figures he meets during the
ascension experience (similar to the heautoscopies of Abulafia
and Har'ar). Notably, the highest magnitude of the technique
provides a way for redemption and the Messiah's arrival, which
will occur when people will be able to perform "the unifications

and the ascents of the soul as you do." This is unique compared with most traditions that induce out-of-body experiences, which have an esoteric character.

MYSTIC 10: YEHUDA ALBOTINI

Yehuda Albotini, an early-sixteenth-century author related to ecstatic Kabbalah and active in Jerusalem, writes in *Sullam ha-ʿAliya:*

> . . . [the mystic] should prepare his true thought to visualize in his heart and mind as if he sits on high, in the heavens of heavens, in front of the Holy One, blessed be He, within the splendor and the radiance of his *Shekhina*. And it is as if he sees the Holy One, blessed be He, sitting as a king. And he should ascend and link and cleave his soul and thought then from one rank to another . . . as far as his power affords, to cause it to cleave and to ascend on high . . . so as to be then as if an intellect in actu, and it has no sense with the sensibilia because it exited the human dominion and then entered the divine dominion.[67]

This description contains elements of autoscopy, as the mystic sees his own image located outside of his bodily borders. The mystic is also described as being in sitting position, as is common with autoscopy. There is a detachment from the "sensibilia," which has more to do with the experience of unification with the "intellect in actu." (In accordance with the Aristotelian tradition, and in contrast to the ascension on high, the unification is with the "intellect in actu" and not with a heavenly figure.) In fact, the autoscopic image of the mystic in front of the "Holy One ... sitting as a king" elucidates the experience of unification since the autoscopic form might mix with the divine form. Similarly to Vital, Albotini mentions an unconscious-like state—"as a dead man." Thus, this description combines elements of autoscopy and ascension on high, common in out-of-body experiences.

MYSTIC 11: DOV BAER OF MEZERITCH

The "Great Maggid" Dov Baer of Mezeritch (1704–1772) was the Besht's main disciple and continued to develop his teachings. In his seminal book *Maggid Devarav le-Ya'aqov* he writes:

> Two halves of forms, as it is written "on the throne, a likeness in the appearance of a man above upon it," as man [that is, *'ADaM*] is but *D* and *M* [*Dam* = blood], and the speech dwells upon him. And when he unites with God, who is the Alpha of this world, he becomes *'ADaM* ... and man must separate himself from any corporeal thing, to such an extent that he will ascend through all the worlds and be in union with God until [his] existence will be annihilated, and then he will be called "*ADaM*."[68]

The Great Maggid paraphrases the unio-mystical ideal as a homily on the verse, "Make thee two trumpets of silver, of a whole piece shall thou make them" (Num 10:2). The Hebrew word for trumpets, *hazozerot*, is interpreted as *hazi-zurot*, that is "[two] half-forms." He states that the man has two half-forms: one is an embodied, corporeal form (DaM), and the other is a disembodied form, which is united with the divine after man manages to "separate himself from any corporeal thing"; that is, the unitive experience culminates with the total loss of the physical form. While the autoscopic form ascends on high, the physical body, represented by the *DaM* (blood), unites with the A (Aleph, Alpha), which represents the divine. The mystic then experiences an intimate unification with the divine. The total detachment of the disembodied form from the physical and "any corporeal thing" is similar to the disembodiment and depersonalization that characterize out-of-body experiences. The experience of elevation also hints at an out-of-body experience. The unification here is double bound in the core of the teaching (the two halves and the *ADaM*) as well as in the experience "when he unites with God." Finally, the auditory component is also mentioned here (already in the original biblical origin of the commentary) as "the speech dwells" on the prophet/mystic, the lofty achievement of the unification experience.

5. Analyzing Mystical Experiences

We now discuss these mystical reports with respect to modern studies on autoscopic phenomena in healthy people and neurological patients. We begin with a phenomenological analysis of the reports and then investigate the various cognitive and neural mechanisms that lie at their base. This might enable further understanding of the mystical approaches and techniques and perhaps the experiences themselves.

PHENOMENOLOGICAL ANALYSIS

Table 1 summarizes the phenomenological results. Two of the accounts described an experience of autoscopy per se (Ibn-Malka and *Sefer ha-Hayim*); four accounts are compatible with

Table 1. Phenomenological Findings: Autoscopy, Heautoscopy, and Out-of-Body Experience

Mystic no.	Name	Autoscopic phenomena	Disembodiment	Depersonalization	Speech	Double's position	Weakness/loss of consciousness
1	Abulafia	Heautoscopy (simultaneous)	–	–	+	Standing	Not reported
2	Har'ar	Heautoscopy (alternated)	–	+	+	Standing	+
3	Ha-Kohen	Heautoscopy (alternated)	+/–	+	+	Not reported	+
4	Isaac of Acre	Heautoscopy (alternated)	–	+	+	Standing	+
5	Qalqish	Heautoscopy (simultaneous)	–	–	+	Standing	Not reported
6	Ibn-Malka	Autoscopic hallucination	–	–	+	Standing	Not reported
7	Sefer ha-Hayim	Autoscopic hallucination	–	–	+	Not reported	+
8	Vital	Out-of-body experience	+	+	Hearing	Supine	+
9	The Besht	Out-of-body experience	+	+	+	Supine	+
10	Albotini	Out-of-body experience/ autoscopic hallucination	+/–	+	–	Sitting	+
11	The Great Maggid	Out-of-body experience	+	+	+	Supine	+

out-of-body experiences, in which the self is experienced to be not only out of the body, but also "ascending on high" to an elevated position (Vital, the Besht, Albotini, the Great Maggid). Five mystics experienced heautoscopy, leading to a combined sensation of autoscopy and unification with the external image (Abulafia, Har'ar, Ha-Kohen, Isaac of Acre, and Qalqish). Seven described verbal communication between the physical and autoscopic bodies (Abulafia, Har'ar, Ha-Kohen, Isaac of Acre, Qalqish, Ibn-Malka, and *Sefer ha-Hayim*). Eight mystics reported explicitly seeing an image of their own self (Abulafia, Har'ar, Ha-Kohen, Isaac of Acre, Qalqish, Ibn-Malka, *Sefer ha-Hayim*, and Vital). Two mystics described light as a prominent feature (Har'ar and *Sefer ha-Hayim*). Five mentioned the position of the autoscopic body, and these five saw their doubles in a standing position (Abulafia, Har'ar, Isaac of Acre, Qalqish, and Ibn-Malka). Three mystics were sitting during the experience (Abulafia, Har'ar, and Isaac of Acre). Five reported an experience of "trembling" (Abulafia, Har'ar, Ha-Kohen, Isaac of Acre, and *Sefer ha-Hayim*), though the sensation of fear was described only among the mystics who described heautoscopy (Abulafia, Har'ar, and Ha-Kohen). Happiness was experienced by three of the mystics (Abulafia, Isaac of Acre, and Ibn-Malka).

CENTRAL CHARACTERISTICS OF MYSTICAL EXPERIENCES: PERSPECTIVE, SELF-LOCATION, AND DEPERSONALIZATION

Autoscopy and heautoscopy are characterized by the experience of a realistic double appearing in front of the mystic. The experiences do not involve disembodiment since the mystic feels himself as residing in the physical body. Heautoscopy is characterized by depersonalization, where self-location is frequently ambiguous, for the mystic could not easily decide whether his self was localized in the physical or in the autoscopic body. Thus, Abulafia and Qalqish experienced seeing the world from their embodied and disembodied perspectives at the same time (simultaneous heautoscopy): as Abulafia put it, "go back as if the one standing opposite you is answering you; and you yourself answer, changing your voice." Har'ar, Ha-Kohen, and Isaac of Acre had the impression that they were alternating between the two positions and perspectives (alternating heautoscopy), along with a feeling of depersonalization while seeing the double ("my self disappeared from me").[69] Both simultaneous and alternating heautoscopy have been described in neurological patients and healthy subjects. Whereas all mystics with alternating heautoscopy experienced depersonalization, mystics with simultaneous heautoscopy preserved their association with the physical body. Clear disembodiment (experience of the self as localized outside one's physical bodily boundaries) was described mostly in out-of-body experiences.

Two accounts (Ibn-Malka and *Sefer ha-Hayim*) described autoscopy, as these mystics felt that their center of awareness remained within their physical bodies and saw their double in an extrapersonal space: "something separate from your body [but] like you." Notably, two mystics who experienced autoscopy stated that the double appeared "as one who sees himself in a mirror." This is typically reported by people experiencing autoscopy of neurological origin. Finally, no mystic who experienced autoscopy reported depersonalization or disembodiment; the first characterizes heautoscopy (and out-of-body experiences), and the second characterizes out-of-body experiences.

Four mystics (Vital, the Besht, Albotini, and the Great Maggid) reported out-of-body experiences; namely, they experienced leaving their own bodies (disembodiment) with a sense of elevation, as is widely reported in patients who have out-of-body experiences. In addition, three of them (Vital, the Besht, and Albotini) reported loss of consciousness or even a cataleptic-like position during the experience. Both are also reported in neurological patients who have the experience during an epileptic seizure.

CHARACTERISTICS OF THE AUTOSCOPIC EXPERIENCE

With regard to the visual characteristics of the autoscopic body during autoscopy and heautoscopy, five mystics reported seeing themselves from the front; that is, the double and the mystic were facing each other (Abulafia, Ha-Kohen, Isaac of Acre, Qalqish, and the author of *Sefer ha-Hayim*); two mystics (Har'ar and Ibn-Malka) reported seeing a back view as well. All of the mystics saw the face of the autoscopic body (their double) as their own face. This has been noted in autoscopic phenomena of psychiatric and neurological origin. However, none of the mystics specifically mentioned seeing other parts of the autoscopic body or seeing their autoscopic body in its entirety. Partialness of the autoscopic body is commonly reported in autoscopic phenomena; the upper body is seen more often than the whole body. Out-of-body experiences also include, in addition to disembodiment, an autoscopic experience from the new, elevated point of view. In the reports presented, the out-of-body experience seems to serve the mystical interest of "ascension on high," but two mystics (Vital and Albotini) mentioned visualization of their physical body and/or its surroundings.

Three mystics described unformed visual sensations of body photism. Nathan Har'ar, for instance, described seeing

light as "it issues from myself." And the experience of seeing a
bright light coming from his or her own body was reported by
a neurological patient as follows: "Light moved from my body
on the floor. It lit up the room ... somehow I became the
light source."[70] The experience of illusory light sources or
radiation("flashes," "white light") is reported in about 30 percent of subjects who had out-of-body experiences or other
autoscopic phenomena.[71]

   With regard to the positions of the physical and autoscopic bodies, two mystics with out-of-body experiences (Vital
and the Besht) mentioned their supine positions during the
experience; one mystic who experienced heautoscopy (Abulafia) mentioned the standing position of the autoscopic body;
one who experienced autoscopy (Qalqish) reported that both
he and the autoscopic body were in seated positions. Patients
who experience autoscopy and heautoscopy tend to see their
doubles in the same position as their physical bodies—standing
or seated—whereas patients with out-of-body experiences tend
to have the experience in a supine position. Thus, the patient's
body position might influence the autoscopic experience, where
sitting or standing positions might lead to autoscopy/heautos-
copy and the supine position to an out-of-body experience.
Here also, mystics who experienced autoscopy/heautoscopy
practiced their techniques while seated, as Abulafia instructed
his followers: "sit as though a man is standing before you."
Mystics who had an out-of-body experience practiced their
techniques in the supine position, which might facilitate the
achievement of this experience.

   Despite their name, autoscopic phenomena are not limited to the visual appearance of an autoscopic body but include
a selective set of other sensory manifestations. The autoscopic phenomena described above were associated with a

variety of nonvisual phenomena. Five mystics reported sensations of "trembling" (Abulafia, Har'ar, Ha-Kohen, Isaac of Acre, and *Sefer ha-Hayim*) as reported in people with autoscopic phenomena. Har'ar associated the effect of the letter-combination method with vestibular manifestations: "letter transposition . . . affects the 'proper' balance of the body, so has this an effect on the soul by the power of the name."[72] Most mystics did not elaborate on locomotive action of the autoscopic body, yet Abulafia saw the double approaching the physical body.

The appearance of the double commonly evoked emotions. Three mystics described the sensation of fear (Abulafia, Har'ar, and Ha-Kohen), and three described a sense of happiness (Abulafia, Isaac of Acre, and Ibn-Malka). Emotional association, with the dominance of fear, is described in the neurological literature. Three mystics (Har'ar, Ha-Kohen, and Isaac of Acre) described surprise at the appearance of the double, as is also described in the neurological literature.[73]

SPEAKING WITH THE DOUBLE

A pattern not widely reported in the neurological literature is the frequent occurrence of auditory manifestations, when the mystics not only saw the double, but also heard the autoscopic body speaking, or, at least, their experience had some auditory character. Indeed, some neurological patients with autoscopy, especially of a long duration, mentioned "talking images" or said that they "heard" their double speaking to them "in their head" or "in their mind." Other forms of auditory phenomena, such as speaking voices not directly related to the autoscopic body, a "beeping sound," the sound of machinery, and undefined voices, have also been reported in the literature. In addition, an auditory analogue to autoscopic phenomena was described: the "hearing of a presence." A pure "hearing of a presence" is characterized by only hearing the double (or another person) close by and not seeing the double, as in autoscopic phenomena. This auditory form was described as the convincing feeling of hearing "a person" behind oneself, who might be nothing but a projection of the experiencer into the extrapersonal space. Another variant was reported by Har'ar, who, at the beginning of his practices, heard a voice emanating from his own body and accompanying the autoscopic phenomena ("speech which emerges from my heart and comes to my lips, forcing them to move").[74]

The experience of a speaking double might result from an additional implication of brain systems related to audition and speech. Interestingly, both auditory and language cortices are localized in close proximity to the anatomical site proposed to be involved in autoscopic phenomena. Alternatively, these phenomenological differences might be related to the artificial induction of a mystical experience, which might therefore be phenomenologically different from a spontaneous mystical experience. The language-based induction method (letter combination and recitation) that the mystics used might also have led to a higher frequency of speaking doubles. Because audition—like vision, balance, and somato-sensation—is involved in constructing the representation of the body in the brain, the experience of a speaking double might be due to an additional interference with auditory mechanisms of own-body perception evoked by the mystical technique. The phenomenology, therefore, cannot be separated from its neurological basis.

6. Autoscopic, Ascension, and Unitive Ecstasies: Different Kabbalistic Trends, Different Brain Mechanisms

DECODING NEUROCOGNITIVE MECHANISMS BEHIND ECSTASY

A main phenomenological distinction among the mystical reports presented here concerns embodiment. Mystics who experienced autoscopy heard the speaking double while residing embodied in their own physical bodies; mystics with out-of-body experiences left their physical bodies (disembodiment) in order to "ascend" on high; and mystics who experienced heautoscopy alternated between the physical and the autoscopic bodies or experienced residing in both simultaneously.

In order to distinguish between neurocognitive mechanisms responsible for embodiment and disembodiment, two different tasks were designed. In one (embodied task), participants were presented with a human figure and were asked to make judgments about the figure's spatial orientation after having imagined that the figure would be their reflection in a mirror (Figure 2c, top). This involved visual body imagery from their own embodied self-location. In a second task (disembodied task), participants were asked to make the same judgments after having imagined themselves to be in the body position of the figure (Figure 2c, bottom), thus mentally imagining themselves in a disembodied self-location.[75] These tasks resemble the mystical techniques described above. In Abulafia's technique, mystics imagined a human figure standing in front of them, as in a mirror (embodied); in Vital's and the Besht's techniques, they imagined themselves as exiting their body (disembodied) and viewing the world from this disembodied self-location.

Electrical neuroimaging applied during task performance showed two brain regions to be implicated in these tasks. The extrastriate body area (EBA, Figure 3) in the lateral occipito-temporal cortex responds selectively to images of human bodies and body parts. This brain area is also activated by imagining bodies and even by the movement of one's own body, suggesting its role in the integration of multisensory body-related information.[76] The temporo-parietal junction (TPJ, Figures 3 and 4) has also been shown to be engaged in integrating multisensory body-related information, including visual, tactile, and proprioceptive input. Moreover, the temporo-parietal junction is involved in various cerebral processes related to the continuous function of the human self, such as egocentric visuo-spatial perspective taking (the ability to look at a scene from different points of view), agency (the capacity to act in the world), the distinction between self and other, theory of mind (the ability to attribute mental states to the self and others), and mental imagery of human bodies.[77]

In-depth analysis showed that activations of the extrastriate body area and the temporo-parietal junction are dependent on embodiment and disembodiment. Tasks involving embodiment activated the extrastriate body area bilaterally, while the disembodiment task activated the right temporo-parietal junction and the left extrastriate body area (Figure 3). Notably, the embodied task involves mostly visual imagery of the subjects as in a mirror, similar to autoscopy. This task shows the back and front views of human figures, resembling Ibn-Malka's description of the mystic who "sees himself front and back, as one who sees himself in a mirror." The same reference is mentioned by Har'ar: "If he is able to compel and to further draw [from his thought] it [the mental image] will emerge from within to without, and it will be imagined for him by the power of his

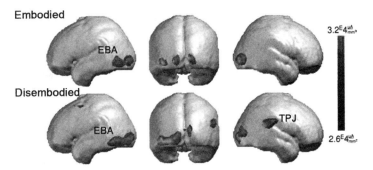

Figure 3. The extrastriate body area (EBA) and the temporo-parietal junction (TPJ). These two brain regions are supposed to be responsible for the integration of multisensory input and for body processing, such as responding to bodies or mental imagery of bodies, agency (being the author of one's own thoughts and actions), visual and perceptual perspective taking, and self-location. Disturbance of the activity in these regions may lead to autoscopic phenomena. Activation of these areas while healthy subjects performed the "embodied" and "disembodied" tasks (Figure 2c) are shown with activation of the EBA bilaterally (top row) and the right TPJ and left EBA (bottom row), respectively (adapted from S. Arzy, G. Thut et al., "Neural basis of embodiment: distinct contributions of temporoparietal junction and extrastriate body area." *J Neurosci* 26 [2006]: 8074–81, used with permission).

purified imagination in the form of a pure mirror, . . . back side is transformed and becomes the front, and he recognizes the nature of its inner side from the outside."[78] As this task mostly involves visual processing of human bodies, it recruits relevant brain mechanisms, namely, the extrastriate body area. The disembodiment task involves not only visual mechanisms, but also mechanisms related to "self-projection" and visuo-spatial perspective taking, therefore recruiting also the temporo-parietal junction where multisensory coding of the human body and self occurs.[79] In addition, these results show that disembodiment relies more on right hemispheric activity, as the right temporo-parietal junction was active for disembodiment and the right extrastriate body area for embodiment. This right hemispheric predominance is concordant with the role of the right hemisphere in self-processing and spatial dispensation.[80]

Clinical studies support these neuroimaging data since patients who have out-of-body experiences generally suffer from brain lesions (frequently epileptic focus) at the temporo-parietal junction, predominantly at the right hemisphere (Figure 4); patients who experience autoscopy/heautoscopy are often found to have an epileptic focus and/or brain lesion at the occipito-temporal cortex and the extrastriate body area. Direct electrical stimulation at the right temporo-parietal junction was reported to induce out-of-body experiences. Taken together, these studies show autoscopy/heautoscopy and out-of-body experiences to rely on brain mechanisms at the extrastriate body area and the temporo-parietal junction, respectively.[81]

Further characteristics of Abulafia's method may be linked to brain mechanisms at the extrastriate body area. The method relies on visual mental imagery of a human form, a function processed at that brain region. Moreover, neurological and neuroimaging studies suggest that mental imagery of reading or expressing letters or phonemes—such as a line orientation task, letter-matching task, letter-case judgment task, or rhyming—as in Abulafia's method, leads to an activation of a mechanism also centered at the occipito-temporal cortex.[82] Given the central role of language and letters in Abulafia's method, it might be hypothesized that this method may modulate activity at the occipito-temporal cortex by the reading and rehearsal of letters. In contrast, the ascension

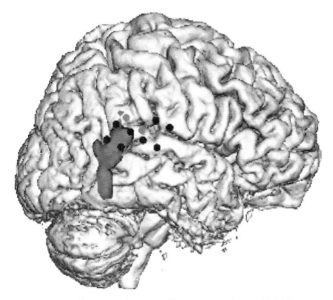

Figure 4. Lesion location in out-of-body experience (OBE) patients. The MRI-based lesion overlap analysis of three OBE patients is shown. In two patients, the OBE site was located by intracranial electrodes (dots) during invasive presurgical epilepsy evaluation and in one patient by noninvasive methods (shade) for localizing the seizure-onset zone. Note the implication of the temporo-parietal junction in all patients (from O. Blanke, T. Landis, L. Spinelli, and M. Seeck, "Out-of-body experience and autoscopy of neurological origin." *Brain* 127 [2004]: 243–58, by permission of Oxford University Press).

technique asks in addition that mystics mentally imagine themselves "on high," changing their habitual visuo-spatial perspective and self-location to a nonhabitual one. This requires activation of brain mechanisms in the right temporo-parietal junction, in a way similar to the disembodiment task.

INDUCING AUTOSCOPIC PHENOMENA

Most mystical and scientific techniques that have been applied to induce autoscopic phenomena used respiration, concentration, and sleep deprivation as a preparatory phase. Mystics who have further used Abulafia's technique mostly experienced autoscopy or heautoscopy, probably owing to several characteristics in that technique. The method combines two components: a verbal one and imagery. To start, the mystic pronounces various syllables of the letter combinations involving reading and speaking. Later phases involve the mental imagery of letters and then human forms, sometimes including mental transformation of these forms as described by Har'ar and Ibn-Malka (the mystic "sees himself front and back, as one who sees himself in a mirror"), similar to the above-described embodiment task. However, the techniques of the Lurianic school used by Vital and the Besht involved mental imagery of the mystic's body changing his habitual self-location while ascending on high, similar to the abovementioned disembodiment task. It is the underlying technique that therefore leads to the particular experience.

The appearance of autoscopy and heautoscopy in Abulafia's technique and out-of-body experiences in the Lurianic method may also owe to the mystic's position during the experience. Clinical observations show that autoscopy and heautoscopy are associated with the experiencer being in a standing or sitting position, whereas out-of-body experiences occur when the experiencer is in a supine position. To further investigate this observation, the abovementioned embodiment and disembodiment tasks were compared in subjects in two different body positions: supine and sitting. Neuroimaging results showed that a change from supine to sitting position modifies brain activity at the extrastriate body area for the embodiment task but does not modify temporo-parietal junction activity during the disembodiment task.[83] These findings correspond with the above techniques, as Abulafia's technique was performed in a sitting position (promoting activity at the extrastriate body area and therefore leading to the experience of autoscopy or heautoscopy), whereas the ascension technique was performed in a supine position (promoting out-of-body experiences, which rely on activity at the temporo-parietal junction). This latter point supports our approach relating the phenomenological characteristics of the mystical experience and its underlying brain activity to the performance of a specific mystical technique.

7. Conclusion

This chapter reviewed the three subtypes of autoscopic phenomena (autoscopy, heautoscopy, and out-of-body experience) compared with three ecstatic mystical experiences: autoscopy, mystical union, and ascension on high. Differences in the induction techniques and the resulting phenomenology of the experiences were compared with experiences measured in the laboratory setting and observed clinically. This allowed phenomenological classification of the mystical experiences in terms used nowadays in cognitive neurology (such as embodiment and disembodiment, visual perspective taking, agency, or ownership). Moreover, activations of distinct brain areas, namely, the temporo-parietal junction and the extrastriate body area, were proposed to underlie the different phenomena. A prominent characteristic of the ecstatic Kabbalah experiences described above is a speaking double. This might be explained by the close vicinity of the extrastriate body area and temporo-parietal cortex to auditory and speech-perception brain areas, activated by the different techniques used in the different mystical trends. Indeed, a large portion of the brain is dedicated to vision, and vision is a major part of the experiential life of humans. However, the assemblage of the senses (multisensory) that gives rise to the subjective experience should not be underestimated. Body-processing and perception, as well as the subjective experience, therefore rely on the integration of several inputs from the external world and from the internal milieu. This integration may nevertheless be disrupted, as we have seen here for bodily consciousness, and we shall see further in the next chapter.

IV

The Spirit in the Brain
Trance and Possession in Jewish Mysticism

1. Dissociative Trance Disorders

Dissociative disorders are among the most mysterious and intriguing phenomena in neuropsychiatry. People with a dissociative disorder dissociate themselves from reality, mostly due to disturbances in the organization of identity, memory, perception, or consciousness. During a dissociative event a fundamental component of the self is separated as people "lose" their self-identity, sometimes identifying themselves with an external agent.[1] Thus, the investigation of dissociative disorders might be valuable for the scientific study of the self. Dissociative disorders have long attracted attention not only in clinical neuropsychiatry, but also in literature (for example, Robert Louis Stevenson's *Strange Case of Dr. Jekyll and Mr. Hyde*, S. Ansky's *The Dybbuk* [Figure 5], and Umberto Eco's *Foucault's Pendulum*) and films (such as *Being John Malkovich* and *The Exorcist*). Dissociative states are also common during mystical experiences, and several mystical schools—including Kabbalah—teach practitioners how to voluntarily induce dissociative states.[2] Therefore, the scientific investigation of dissociative disorders might shed new light on dissociation during mystical experience and on our understanding of the concept of the "self." In particular, the voluntary induction of a phenomenon related to a psychiatric disorder might illuminate the continuity of the psychiatric scale from healthy subjects through personality disorders to psychiatric patients.[3]

Dissociative disorders include dissociative amnesia (when memories are not consciously accessible), dissociative fugue (detachment from the immediate environment or memory, sometimes resulting in sudden travel away from home), depersonalization disorder (a feeling of detachment from one's body), dissociative identity disorder (formerly known as multiple personality disorder, that is, dissociation in identity components leading to a combination of different identities), and dissociative trance disorder. Dissociative trance disorder has been divided into two broad categories: trance and possession. Trance is characterized by a sudden alteration in consciousness, accompanied by distinct alternative identities. It might be accompanied by a narrowing of one's awareness of immediate surroundings, stereotyped behaviors, and movements experienced as being beyond one's control. The symptoms and signs of trance are rather simple and usually include sudden collapse, immobilization, dizziness, and shrieking, screaming, or crying; memory is rarely affected. In contrast, possession frequently involves sudden extreme changes in sensory and motor control, including replacement of the customary sense of personal identity by a new identity, attributed to the influence of a spirit, power, deity, or other person. Affected individuals might

Figure 5. Sasha Demidov (left) as Hanan and Efrat Ben-Zur (middle) as Leah in *The Dybbuk*, directed by Y. Arye, based on the 1914 play by S. Ansky. Here, Leah is being possessed by a dibbuq, or malicious spirit of a dead person—an example of a dissociative disorder. Photo: Daniel Kaminsky; Gesher Theatre, Israel 2014 (used with permission).

shake convulsively, hyperventilate, scream, and exhibit agitation and aggressive movements. These may be followed by collapse and a loss of consciousness. Subsequently, such individuals report being exhausted and may have amnesia regarding the event.[4]

Dissociative trance disorders are ubiquitous all over the world, yet their makeup differs among cultures. In the Western world most dissociative disorders are not specified, and the different subtypes are evenly distributed across the dissociation spectrum; in non-Western countries trance and possession are common diagnoses. Examples include the *ataque de nervios*, which was found in 12 percent of the healthy population in Puerto Rico and is also abundant in other parts of Latin America; the *lata* in Malaya, where individuals may have a sudden vision of a spirit threatening them; the *jinn* in Muslim countries; and a possession syndrome in India during which affected individuals suddenly begin to speak in an altered voice with a new identity, usually that of a deity recognizable to others. Through this voice they might refer to themselves in the third person, and they may negotiate for changes in the family environment or society or become agitated or aggressive. Different cultures also distinguish between voluntary and involuntary possession. In the Haitian Vodou religion, possession is perceived as an involuntary illness that should be cured by shamanistic exorcism; however, possession also might be induced intentionally in ritual religious contexts.[5]

Individuals who suffer from dissociative disorders are easily hypnotized and sensitive to cultural or religious influence. Women make up the majority of cases, up to 90 percent in some studies. Trauma has been suggested as contributing to the development of dissociative symptoms, particularly sexual and physical abuse in childhood and in patients with borderline personality disorder and other "Cluster B" (narcissistic, histrionic, or antisocial) disorders. This background might be related to the sexual content frequently described in dissociative disorders. And research regarding survivors of life-threatening events indicates that more than half of dissociative phenomena include a sense of detachment or unreality, automatic movements, or depersonalization; these presentations are supposed to be adaptive defenses against such traumatic situations.[6]

The term *désagrégation* (originally designated by P. Janet) might be applicable to dissociative disorders. Normally, different events are experienced as connected to one another, but in dissociative states they are experienced as isolated from other mental processes. Thus, dissociative disorders are not a disturbance in the perceptions themselves or their content but in their organization or integration. When memories are separated, the dissociation is called dissociative amnesia. Fragmentation of identity results in dissociative identity disorder. Disintegrated perception is characteristic of depersonalization disorder, and dissociation of consciousness appears in various possession and dissociative trance disorders. Hence, patients with dissociative identity disorder suffer not from too many personalities, but from having less than one integrated personality. To reiterate: it is suggested that the core problem in dissociative disorders involves information processing—the failure to integrate mental elements rather than their content.[7]

2. Maggid and Dibbuq

In Kabbalistic literature since the late fifteenth century, we find two main forms of trance and possession: the maggid and the dibbuq. The term "dibbuq" is used in Jewish mysticism to designate a spirit of a dead person that takes temporary possession of a human being by inhabiting the body of the possessed individual. The possession is characterized by a striking down of the subject's body, accompanied by convulsions and a change in voice, behavior, and personality, and sometimes by the expression of further knowledge or speech in a language apparently unknown to the subject. The term "maggid" is used to indicate "a celestial entity" that takes over the mystic's mental state, "delivering" mystical secrets to the Kabbalist. A maggid experience involves the alternation of consciousness and subjective experiences perceived as being beyond one's control and is thus close to the trance state. It has been attributed to males and has been evaluated as a source of reliable religious information. Dibbuq possession, in contrast, has been attributed to both men and women and has been seen as negative since the possessing spirit is portrayed as a sinner. Yet in both cases there is a separation between one's habitual self and the dissociated self, which might express knowledge, memory, and behaviors unknown to the habitual self. This distinction is reminiscent of William James's categories of demoniac or "low" mysticism versus "higher" forms of mystical experiences.[8]

Possession and trance experiences have usually been neglected or marginalized in neuroscientific studies and mostly have been treated in traditional myths and literature. In Jewish culture these phenomena have been investigated mainly through the psychocultural work of Yoram Bilu and through sociological, historical, and religious studies found in works by Raphael Patai, Matt Goldish, and Yossi Chajes. Outside Jewish studies, psychodynamic and sociological explanations of the phenomena have been suggested.[9] Possession and other dissociative disorders have been widely described, obviously, in psychiatric literature. Not much has been done, however, to help in the understanding of the neurocognitive mechanisms underlying dissociative phenomena, namely, how a person might express behaviors and characteristics seemingly alien to his habitual self. The descriptions of distinct Jewish mystics about their self-induced dissociative experiences might serve as a valuable contribution for such an investigation, as specific techniques led to certain experiences. Here we compare reports of Kabbalistic experiences with phenomenological evidence found in anthropological reports and psychiatric cases as well as with new discoveries regarding the functional and anatomical mechanisms of memory and consciousness. We consider as ecstatic experiences those induced by specific practices that aimed to evoke experiences of altered consciousness. According to the terminology defined above, an ecstatic experience will therefore refer more to a maggidic experience (or a dissociative experience with maggidic elements), for the maggid was intentionally induced in order to reveal mystical secrets to the Kabbalist.

3. The Maggid and Its Induction

As a technical term, "maggid" is known in Jewish literature in the medieval *Sefer ha-Tamar*, which is a translation of an Arabic source.[10] Maggid phenomena were also common in the circle of *Sefer ha-Meshiv* in Spain. Rabbi Joseph Taitatzak of this circle brought the maggidic tradition to Thessalonica and Constantinople. Maggidic tradition was also widespread in Safedian Kabbalah, including its main practitioners, such as rabbis Isaac Luria, Hayim Vital, and Moshe Cordovero, as well as Joseph Karo, who was reported by other Kabbalists to have had a maggid experience. Other known cases are those of rabbis Menahem Azaria of Fano, Aaron Berakhiah of Modena (a student of Azaria), David Habillio, Moshe Zacut, Samson of Ostropol, and Moshe Hayim Luzzatto.[11]

Perhaps the most famous maggid experience in Jewish tradition was attributed to Rabbi Joseph Karo (1488–1575). Although mostly known for his monumental halachic monographs *Beit Yosef* and *Shulkhan Aruch*, Karo, remarkably, did not show special concern in his mystical diary *Maggid Meisharim* about his halachic work. This might hint at the higher importance he attributed to his dissociative revelation. As seen in *Maggid Meisharim*, Karo was fascinated by memory functions and used memory exercises (recitation of long memorized paragraphs of the Mishnah) to induce his maggidic-like experiences, mostly reported as automatic speech: "Behold the voice of my beloved knocketh in my mouth and the lyre sounded of itself."[12] Much more often, the power revealed to

Karo, which in the vast majority of the cases is a feminine entity known as the *Shekhinah* (the feminine dwelling or settling presence of God), the Mishnah (the first major redaction into written form of Jewish oral traditions), or the Soul, states that "I am talking to you as a man to his friend"; this might be related to the above-discussed "speaking *Doppelgänger*" (see chapter 3). Yet Karo could never see his mentor and always reports the revealing power as speaking "in his mouth." The same is reported by Rabbi Moshe Hayim Luzzatto, who never saw his maggid, stating that "I could hear his voice speaking in my mouth."[13] The description by Rabbi Moshe Cordovero, one of the important figures of Safedian Kabbalah of the sixteenth century, points to speech as the feature distinguishing between the phenomena of the maggid and the dibbuq: "man can be entered by another soul—a holy or an evil—and similarly we have seen demons or evil spirits entering men and troubling them . . . similarly an angel may enter man and speak within him words of wisdom, and this is what is generally called Maggid."[14]

The maggid experience is likely to be induced by two steps. First are preparations, which include, among other things, fasting, sensory deprivation, and mortification as well as penance and abstinence. Thus, Luzzatto would "prepare himself for three days . . . by taking ritual baths and other things designed to appease the Maggidic angel who was speaking to him."[15] In contrast to this individual complex process, possession appears either spontaneously or as preceded by drumming, singing, dancing, or other crowd contagion. Second, the preparations are followed by repetitive and intense recitation of spiritual verses or passages of the Mishnah or divine names.[16] The recitation technique is explained in a passage preserved in Rabbi Israel ben Sabbatai, known as the Maggid of Kuznitz (which means the preacher of Kozienice), in his *Sefer 'Avodath Yisra'el* (written early in the nineteenth century):

> I have heard it said that the holy Rabbi, our teacher Rabbi Gershon [of Kitov] once said this to our master Rabbi Israel Baal Shem Tov, of blessed memory, "As long as you are able to recite voluntarily in your prayers the words 'Blessed are Thou' you should know that you have not yet attained the ideal of prayer. For when he prays a man must be so stripped that it is impossible for him to find the energy and the intellectual activity to speak the words of the prayers." This is perfectly true. Yet there is a still higher truth. This is when a man is stripped of all corporeality, of every kind of will, and is bound only to his Creator, so that he no longer knows how to recite his prayers because of the awe he experiences and because of his attachment to God, yet nonetheless he recites his prayers in the right order. This is because heaven has pity on him, endowing him with speech and the power to pray, as it is said [Psalms 51:17]: "O Lord, open my lips."[17]

4. Personal Reports of Mystical Dissociative Experiences

Here we describe the dissociative, maggid-like experiences of four Kabbalists from the fifteenth and sixteenth centuries. They use well-defined techniques, and their writings are instructive, leading the performer through the sensations they experienced.

MYSTIC 1: JOSEPH KARO

Rabbi Joseph Karo was born in Spain and left with the exiles of 1492 to Constantinople and Adrianople, settling finally in Safed. There he wrote his most famous books, *Beit Yosef* and *Shulkhan Aruch*, but he also participated in the Kabbalistic circle that included Rabbi Moshe Cordovero. His dissociative experience began on the vigil of Shavuot night, when in commemoration of the giving of the Torah on this date, all-night Torah study is customary. Rabbi Shlomo Alkabetz, another famous Kabbalistic figure, reported Karo's experience in an epistle:

> Know that the saint [Karo] and I . . . agreed to stay up all night in order to banish sleep from our eyes on Shavuot. We succeeded, thank God, so that as you will hear, we ceased not from study for even a moment . . . all this we did in dread and awe, with quite unbelievable melody and tunefulness . . . no sooner had we studied two tractates of the *Mishnah* than our Creator smote us so that we heard a voice speaking out of the mouth of the saint, may his light shine. It was a loud voice with letters clearly enunciated. All the companions heard the voice but were unable to understand what was said. It was an exceedingly pleasant voice, becoming increasingly strong. We all fell upon our faces and none of us had any spirit left because of our great dread and awe. The voice began to address us, saying: "friends, choicest of choice, peace to you, beloved companions . . . behold, I am the *Mishnah*, the mother who chastises her children and I have come to converse with you."[18]

This report describes an experience of trance. As a consequence of the mystic reciting the Mishnah, preceded by sleep deprivation, a speaking voice appears, heard also by those in the mystic's surroundings. This appearance seems to be unexpected yet is perceived by the mystic and others as positive. It was not accompanied by catalepsy, and it happened in public. Although the description here is not provided by Karo himself, his various references in *Maggid Meisharim* to his maggidic-like experiences reveal that he remembered the experiences and even wrote them down.

MYSTIC 2: HAYIM VITAL

The ecstatic experiences of Rabbi Hayim Vital are detailed in his mystical diary *Sefer ha-Hezionoth*, where a report of his experience of the maggid appears. It occurred on 30 August 1571 after his teacher Isaac Luria (Ha'Ari) had instructed him to fast for forty-eight hours and to perform a long and complex Yichud (literally, unification—a mystical technique including the recitation of a prayer and the practice of letter combination) over this time. He then reports his experience:

> On the day before Rosh Hodesh Elul [the first day of the twelfth month of the Jewish year, a time of preparation for the High Holy Days] in the year 5331 [1571], my master of blessed memory sent me to the cave of Abaye and Rava [two renowned Babylonian Talmud scholars, living ca. 300–350 CE], and I stretched myself over the grave of Abaye ... first I performed the Yichud of mouth and nose of the Ancient Holy one, and sleep fell upon me. Then I awakened and saw nothing. Afterwards, I once again

stretched myself over the grave of Abaye and performed the Yichud written by my teacher himself.
While combining and interlacing the letters YHVH
[the Tetragrammaton—the name of God] and
ADNY [the construct form of "Adon" (my Lord)], as
is known, my concentration became confused and I
was unable to combine them, and I was refrained
from thinking out this combination. Then within
my consciousness there came a likeness as if a
voice was telling me "retract, retract!" ... so then I
returned to concentrate on the combination and
completed it successfully.... Afterwards, a great and
exceeding fright and trembling seized me in all my
limbs, and my hands were trembling, knocking
against one another, and also my lips were trembling
in an exaggerated way and were moving rapidly with
forcefulness exceedingly fast. It was as if a voice was
sitting on my tongue which was saying exceedingly
swiftly "what shall I say, what shall I say?" more than
one hundred times. And I was trying to take hold of
myself and my tongue so as not to move them, but I
was not able to quiet them at all. Afterwards I
thought to ask for wisdom. And the sound exploded
in my mouth and tongue and said more than twenty
times "the wisdom, the wisdom." Then it went on to
say: "the wisdom and knowledge" many many times
... all this was with great wondrous speed, many
times in the waking state. And I had fallen on my
face, spread out on the grave of Abaye.[19]

This long and detailed report is another classic example
of trance. The experience begins with preparation composed

of fasting and sleep deprivation. The mystic carefully performs in solitude the technique of Yichud as instructed, combining both memory exercises (recitation) and letter combination. Then an intense feeling of fear and trembling gripped the mystic's whole body while he is "spread out" on a grave. The mystic also emphasizes that the experience took place "in a waking state." Only then does the maggidic voice, which the mystic clearly remembered, appear.

MYSTIC 3: NATHAN OF GAZA

Nathan Benjamin ben Elisha ha-Levi, known as Nathan of Gaza (1643–1680), was the main prophet of the messianic Sabbatean movement. His first major prophecy about the messianic mission of Sabbatai Zevi occurred in 1665 as a prophetic vision that lasted twenty-four hours. The vision was not a spontaneous event but rather an experience that Nathan of Gaza intentionally prepared for and induced on Shavuot night (as in Karo's experience). Then he publicly experienced a dissociative state. The full account of this event is given in Baruch of Arezzo's *Zikaron li-Bnei Israel:*

> When the holiday of Shavuot arrived, Rabbi Nathan called the scholars of Gaza to study Torah with him the entire night. And it occurred that in the middle of the night a great sleep fell on Rabbi Nathan; and he stood on his feet and walked back and forth in the room and recited the entire [Mishnah] tractate *Ketubot* by heart. He then asked one of the scholars to sing a certain hymn; then he asked another of the scholars [to do so] . . . meanwhile he leaped and danced in the room, shedding

one piece of clothing after another until his under-
clothes alone remained. He then took a great leap
and fell flat on the ground. When the rabbis saw
this, they wished to help him and to stand him up,
but they found he was like a dead man. . . . Pres-
ently a voice was heard . . . a voice emitted from his
mouth, but his lips did not move. And he said:
"take care concerning my beloved son, my messiah
Sabbatai Zevi"; and it said further, "take care concerning my beloved son, Nathan the Prophet." . . .
afterwards he rested a great rest and began to move
himself. His colleagues helped him to stand up on
his feet and asked him how it had happened and
what he had spoken; he replied that he did not
know anything. The sages told him everything that
had happened, at which he was very amazed.[20]

This intentional event occurred on a sleepless night and
is described as being induced by the recitation of the Mishnah.
This led to a complex of motor activities (dancing, stripping),
which was then followed by cataplexy (loss of muscle tone).
Then the maggidic voice appeared. The mystic consequently
presented with complete amnesia (loss of memory) regarding
the event. This event is probably a case of dissociative disorder,
as it seems that Nathan of Gaza experienced a disturbance
in at least three of the things that characterize such disorders:
a disruption in the organization of identity, memory, perception, or consciousness. However, it was not a clear trance experience, as it also involved some elements of possession. Trance
is characterized by a sudden alteration in consciousness, accompanied by distinct alternative identities, usually involving
sudden collapse and immobilization, as in the current case. In

trance, however, memory is rarely affected, unlike the current case. Here, the content of the experience is perceived as positive, as in trance. Its "heavenly" origin is emphasized by the description of the "voice" as "emitted from his mouth" without the lips moving. Possession mostly involves some amnesia of the event and occurs in public, as here, but it frequently involves sudden extreme changes in sensory and motor control, such as convulsive shaking, hyperventilation, screaming, agitation, and aggressive movements, which might then be followed by collapse and loss of consciousness. Although his experience was not so severe, Nathan of Gaza showed some eccentric behavior, including dancing and stripping, followed by a cataplectic state. These suggest that the described experience is probably a dissociative trance disorder yet one involving components of both trance and possession, which fit the public character of the largest and most influential messianic movement in Jewish history, that is, the Sabbatean movement.

MYSTIC 4: JOSEPH IBN-TSUR

The maggidic experience of Rabbi Joseph ibn-Tsur, a Sabbatean prophet active in northern Africa,[21] is detailed in a letter from Rabbi Abraham ben-Amram to Rabbi Benjamin Duran, describing an investigation of Ibn-Tsur's experiences:

> He [Ibn-Tsur] answered me: "I do not know who speaks with me, neither do I myself see or speak. Rather, my lips move and the speech comes out of them, which produces the sound I hear." I said to him: "With all this are you not able to ask?" He answered: "All my senses are extinguished, and I do not know even if I am in heaven or on earth." He

[said he] wished to open his eyes but was unable, as
if there was lead upon them … it was clear to us
that neither an evil spirit nor a shade was involved
since he was in excellent possession of his senses,
and all his words concerned God's unity, and he
fasted constantly.[22]

This is an experience of trance. Ibn-Tsur is known to have
"fasted constantly," yet this report does not mention a specific
induction technique. He is not able to execute motor activities
besides the expression of the voice. There is a feeling that all
of his senses "are extinguished." It is not reported whether the
event occurred in public or in private; the mystic himself reports
his experience, so it therefore did not involve amnesia. Note
that in this description, the mystic's lips are reported to move,
unlike the description of Nathan of Gaza but similar to the
moving tongue of Vital.

PHENOMENOLOGICAL SUMMARY

Table 2 summarizes these four mystical experiences. Three
mystics had a proper experience of trance, and one, Nathan of
Gaza, experienced a mixture of trance and possession. All mystics exclusively described speaking voices, which came out of
their mouths. This auditory experience was not accompanied
by other hallucinations. The mystics prepared themselves by
fasting and sleep deprivation and induced the experiences by
repetitive incantation of prayers and/or passages from the
Mishnah. Two experiences were accompanied by motor activity (Karo, Vital), and the other two were not (the mystics stayed
still; Nathan of Gaza, Ibn-Tsur). Two mystics (Nathan of Gaza,
Karo) had their experience in public, and another reported it

as occurring in solitude (Vital). Three mystics—Karo, Vital, and Ibn-Tsur—remembered the event, but the fourth, Nathan of Gaza, experienced amnesia.

5. Maggid, Dibbuq, and the Brain

CHARACTERISTICS OF THE MAGGIDIC EXPERIENCE

The maggidic experience in Jewish mysticism is willingly induced by a preparative phase of food and sleep deprivation and then by techniques of Yichud, repetitive incantation of Mishnah or prayers, and sometimes additional techniques such as letters pronounced or mentally imagined in combination or recitation of divine names. The most important characteristic of the maggid experience, in contrast to dibbuq possession, is the content of the messages, which both the mystic and those around him regard as revelations of a sacred entity. In most instances the maggid is exclusively expressed as a voice that uncontrollably emerges from the mystic's throat although it might be accompanied by other hallucinations, which are sometimes close to autoscopic phenomena. This might occur publicly or in solitude; however, in solitude the mystic must be aware of his revelation and remember it, whereas in public he might be amnesic to his dissociative phenomenon. In addition, the experience might be accompanied by various emotions, such as fear or happiness, as well as executive and motor actions that might range from weakness and heaviness to exhibitive activities such as undressing or dancing.

It is interesting to compare these experiences with the above-described autoscopic phenomena (chapter 3), which were also induced voluntarily by ecstatic mystics: in both cases, voices spoke, but in autoscopic phenomena the mystic heard

Table 2. Phenomenological Findings: Trance and Possession

Mystic no.	Name	Dissociative disorder	Preparation	Induction	Motor symptoms	Speaking voice	Loss of consciousness	Public	Amnesia
1	Karo	Trance	Sleep deprivation	Mishnah recitation	–	+	–	+	–
2	Vital	Trance	Fasting, sleep deprivation	Yihud recitation, letter combinations	Severe trembling	+	Falling on his face	–	–
3	Nathan of Gaza	Trance-possession	Sleep deprivation, other	Mishnah recitation	Dancing, stripping	+	+	+	+
4	Ibn-Tsur	Trance	Fasting	Not reported	Unable to move	+	"All my senses are extinguished"	Not reported	–

the speaking voice as coming out of the autoscopic image, whereas here the voice came out of the mystic's mouth; in autoscopic phenomena people experience having two bodies and one self, whereas here two selves inhabit one body; both experiences involve emotions, especially fear accompanied by trembling; finally, both are induced by the use of sleep deprivation and letter combination, yet here mystics used more memorization and recitation techniques, whereas in autoscopic phenomena they mostly pronounced letters and mentally rotated letters and images.

THE INDIVIDUAL CHARACTER OF THE MAGGID AND THE DIBBUQ

Spirit possession is a widespread belief found in various patterns in many countries and traditions—up to 74 percent of a sample of 488 societies worldwide.[23] The maggid and the dibbuq are distinct in their individual characters. The maggid, which is a phenomenon induced by private recitation and the practice of certain techniques, was celebrated; the dibbuq, however, was considered to be demonic and was never experienced within the ceremonial context of a possession cult.[24] Specifically, the distinction between the maggid and the dibbuq is based on the nature of the presented experience. The maggid is considered a positive spirit, whereas the dibbuq is a negative one. Consequently, the maggid was mostly induced privately by the mystic in order to experience an ecstatic revelation and is therefore found among most central mystical figures. The dibbuq is conceived as an evil spirit that unwillingly possesses a naïve individual who then goes through a process of exorcism. Maggidic experiences are mostly remembered by mystics, who may then write them down; dibbuq possession is not remembered by the person having the experience. Here we described the maggid experience mostly as a dissociative trance and the dibbuq as possession. Nevertheless, as the nature of the spirit mainly defines the experience, a maggid might not fit the classical definitions of trance but might also involve components of possession, such as amnesia (as in the description of Nathan of Gaza), while still being considered a maggid.

THE MAGGID AND CONSCIOUSNESS

Much of human mental and cognitive activity is unconscious in the sense of being inaccessible to phenomenal awareness. Examples are automatic processing (exercised activities performed without awareness), procedural memory (memorizing how to perform skilled activities such as driving or riding a bicycle), subliminal perception (processing of stimuli perceived before being consciously approached), or hypnosis (performance of activities or failure to remember certain experiences following appropriate suggestion). These exemplify the fact that consciousness is not an obligatory property of cognitive activity but an experience that might accompany it.[25] It might be suggested that during maggidic trance and possession, some mental activities inaccessible to phenomenal awareness are expressed.

Some researchers, however, suggest regarding consciousness not as awareness of mental states, but rather as a state in which people are able to integrate their self with the objective world outside of that self. This integration creates what is normally perceived as "reality." During dissociative states the normally integrative functions of identity, memory, or consciousness are disturbed (or altered), whereas varying degrees of disruption in information integration across behavioral states underlie the larger failures of integration of the self and certain cognitive faculties in dissociation. The disintegration is expressed as events or perceptions that would ordinarily be connected but during dissociative states become separated. Another explanation is that during dissociative states continuous self-processing is not available to consciousness since two or more information processors operate in parallel without sharing mutual influence.[26] This conscious/unconscious duality may rely on a combination of explicit and implicit memories, sometimes resulting in dissociative disorders.

MAGGIDIC PHENOMENA AND MEMORY

Memory plays a central role in dissociative disorders. In dissociation, two or more distinct identities or personality states repeatedly "take control" of a person's behaviors while different levels of amnesia appear between switches.[27] In fact, different mechanisms of memories are differently related to conscious experience. Memory traces might be activated and used unconsciously. Specifically, while performing a certain procedure, a person may use previous knowledge about the procedure without awareness of this use. Such kinds of memory include "implicit memory" (with regard to its unconscious character) and "procedural memory" (with regard to its application mostly on procedural performance) since it allows learning skills and knowing how to perform actions. Memory traces that are activated and treated consciously—or explicit memory— might be divided into two main groups: semantic memory and autobiographical or episodic memory. Semantic memory is defined as "a network of associations and concepts that underlies our basic knowledge of the world—word meanings, categories, facts and propositions, and the like." This does not render subjective experience but rather objective personal information, which might sometimes partially overlap with implicit memory. Autobiographical memory concerns subjective experience and "allows us explicitly to recall the personal incidents that uniquely define our lives."[28]

Although autobiographical memory seems to be conscious by its very nature, only a certain part of these memories is conscious. Various states, such as hypnosis, or neuropsychiatric disorders, such as posttraumatic stress disorder (PTSD), demonstrate that autobiographical memories might influence daily life without being consciously approached.[29] During dissociative states, autobiographical details not included in the internal world of the subject are expressed. This has to do with the complicated process of memory: memories are not simply being stored but rather reexperienced in the process of retrieval and recollection. This process might be repressed by certain traumatic experiences, leading to change in the activity of brain systems that govern one's self-related mental processing, including autobiographical memory.[30] Moreover, disturbance of autobiographical memory may lead to a vital reexperience of "memories" that have in fact never been experienced, such as "false memories" and confabulations. Patients with such confabulations cannot distinguish between memories and non-memories, acting on the basis of previous habits rather than of currently relevant memories. They do not forget memories but "remember" subjective episodic events that they have never experienced.[31] Here again, the mechanism typically attributed to confabulations is a repression of the retrieval of stored episodic memories. In summary, memory, and especially autobiographical memory, cannot be separated from the "owner" of the autobiography, that is the experiencer. When disintegration appears, it may result in a dissociative state.

INDUCTION OF DISSOCIATIVE DISORDER

A cognitive experiment might shed light on the induction of dissociation. Memory function in patients with dissociative identity disorder was compared with that in two different control groups: a group of healthy subjects and a group of "simulators." These simulators were healthy subjects as well, who were asked to make up an imaginary identity and to "switch" to this second identity during the experiment. Participants were given a seventeen-item data sheet for the "new" identity on which they were asked to assign name, age, sex, physical description, personal history, and personality style. In a procedural memory task (a sequential pattern of button pressing), patients with dissociative identity disorder improved their performance during the task, yet they lost this learned improvement when changing to their second identity. Simulators demonstrated a similar effect of "losing" the learned procedural memory when consciously changing their identity to their new invented one; this effect was not shown in the control group.[32] This suggests that a conscious change in explicit memory (inter-identities) causes a change in implicit memory (performance). To reiterate, a conscious identity change in a healthy subject might lead not only to adoption of another identity, but also to expression of implicit performances of this second identity. These results might serve as a cognitive basis for the induction of maggidic experience.

Descriptions such as "fright and trembling seized me in all my limbs, and my hands were trembling," as reported by Vital, may also resemble ecstatic seizure. Ecstatic seizures are trancelike experiences in which patients may have a heightened sense of self-awareness or joy as an "aura" that may proceed a full seizure.[33] Epilepsy, which may trigger autoscopic phenomena, may lead to a sense of trance, and may further be induced by sleep deprivation or other manipulations that increase susceptibility for a seizure, some of them used by ecstatic mystics. While we cannot exclude such an entity in mystical experiences, no direct evidence supports an entity of epilepsy in the mystics described here.

FUNCTIONAL NEUROANATOMY OF THE MAGGID AND THE DIBBUQ

Different kinds of memories are coded in different anatomical structures of the brain. Procedural memory is coded at first in cortical areas, such as the premotor cortex (representing the executive character of this kind of memory) and the inferior parietal lobule (representing its proximity to semantic memory). After a certain period of practicing, this memory is also transferred and coded in subcortical areas, including the basal ganglia and the cerebellum. Autobiographical memory, however, is coded directly in the hippocampus, at the medial temporal lobe. Bilateral hippocampal lesion is thus characterized by losing the ability to code new autobiographical memory.[34]

Memory processing involves not only encoding processes, but also, and not less importantly, maintenance and retrieval processes, which are also controlled by specific brain regions in the autobiographical memory network (Figure 6). The prefrontal cortex plays an important role in a brain network which underlies a special kind of autonoetic consciousness that allows humans to be aware of past events and to plan their futures.[35] Such cross-temporal contingencies are necessary for facilitating an integrated sense of self between the "I," the core of the subject, the organizer and interpreter of the continuous experience over time, and more external circles, including the body, the environment, and social interactions.[36] The prefrontal cortex plays a key role in temporally organizing and integrating these perceptions into one context-independent self over time. The prefrontal cortex is also known to be involved in conscious experience and self-referential mental activity as well as in explicit representation of states of the self. Furthermore, inhibitory control of information, processed in the orbito-frontal cortex (part of the prefrontal cortex), is crucial for organizing one's behavior over time since new information might otherwise detract from organizing certain behaviors. This inhibitory function protects and complements the integrative functions of memory. The orbito-frontal cortex is primarily responsible for this inhibitory control as it monitors the environment through connections with different multisensory associative cortices. Moreover, there is substantial neuropsychological evidence that the orbito-frontal cortex controls disorganizing interference through inhibitory processes, and causal evidence from lesion studies shows that orbito-frontal lesion might lead to intellectual and emotional disinhibition. Since a hallmark of dissociative disorders is inhibition of a certain part of the conscious subjective experience, the prefrontal and especially the orbito-frontal cortex might play a central role in trance and possession.[37]

Another brain region that plays a major role in memory processing, especially in autobiographical memory, is the posterior parietal cortex, adjacent to and overlapping the temporo-parietal junction. The posterior parietal cortex is divided into the superior parietal lobule, associated with top-down processes that support retrieval search, monitoring, and verification, and the inferior parietal cortex, which is related more to recollection. Studies showed an involvement of the temporo-

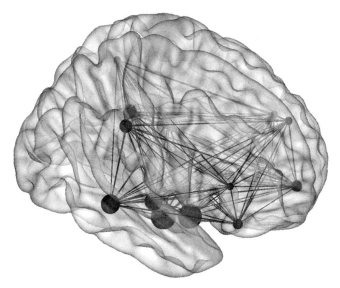

Figure 6. Episodic memory network. The centers of the identified regions are presented on a three-dimensional image produced by magnetic resonance imaging, and the significant connections between them are shown. Region sizes correspond to the average connectivity to the rest of the network. Note the role of the temporo-parietal junction (left) and the frontal (right) and medial temporal (bottom) cortices (adapted with permission from M. Peer et al., "Reversible functional connectivity disturbances during transient global amnesia." *Ann Neurol* 75, 5 [2014]: 634–43. Copyright © 2014 American Neurological Association. Published by John Wiley and Sons).

parietal junction in the maintenance and retrieval of autobiographical memory. The temporo-parietal junction was also found to contribute to "episodic memory thinking" and "mental time travel" of the self "traveling" back and forth in time in order to recall the past and predict the future: the self's referral to past memories and possible future occurrences. As already discussed in chapter 3, the temporo-parietal junction has been shown to be involved in many self- and body-related processes, such as visuo-spatial perspective taking, mental own-body imagery, embodiment, and own-action recognition.[38] Moreover, disruption of activity at the temporo-parietal junction has led to an experience of the "feeling of a presence." This is an experience in which people may have the sensation that somebody is nearby when no one is actually present and cannot be seen. Experimental manipulations have demonstrated that this "presence" is indeed a projection of the subject's own self into the peri-personal space. This may be further considered as a somatosensory version of autoscopic phenomena.[39] Though trance and possession classically do not include clear body reduplication, some trance descriptions may include the "feeling of a presence" of the maggid before the trance and may therefore be related to this kind of reduplication. Although memory as used in the maggidic techniques is mostly procedural and not autobiographical, alteration of the temporo-parietal junction might link the bodily manifestations and memory processes that accompany the maggid experience.

6. Maggid and Dibbuq: Two Selves in One Person

Dissociative disorders challenge the ordinary corporeal experience as two "selves" are held in one body, in contrast to autoscopic phenomena, in which one self has two different bodies (feeling of a presence may represent an intermediate form). Two different forms of dissociative disorders are found in Jewish mysticism—the maggid and the dibbuq. While the dibbuq is experienced as a spontaneously occurring unwilled disturbance (and thus is perceived as a mental illness that should be exorcized), the maggid is perceived as an ecstatic experience. This experience is intentionally induced by specific techniques aimed at getting the practicing mystic into the emanation of a "speaking voice" from his throat that reveals materials unavailable in his "original," or "non-maggidic," state of mind. By challenging memory capacities (and other components of the memory network) through the precise performance of the mystical technique, the mystic manages to interfere with the regular stream of conscious-explicit and unconscious-implicit memories to "create" another personality that denounces his "original" one by opposing different subjective contents and reflections. Together with autoscopic phenomena or the feeling of a presence, dissociative trance disorders propose that body and self might be related in ways not necessarily reflecting habitual perception; such experiences might therefore be of exceptional value to mystics interested in in-depth investigation of their own selves. Even nowadays, dissociative states might present a valuable advantage to consciousness studies and to the neuropsychological understanding of the human "self."

Conclusions

1. Some Final Methodological Remarks

The present study is part of an effort to widen the methodological tools that should be used in understanding the complexities characterizing the experiences reflected in Kabbalistic and other mystical literature. Such an effort is sometimes the result of conversations between scholars from different fields, conversations which may open some aspects of Kabbalistic literature to fresh understandings that produce new perspectives—if done in a cautious manner. The need to address this literature from many perspectives is an imperative that has been stressed several times in recent studies.[1] In addition to the classical methods—the philological and the historical—new methods should be welcomed. Modern approaches of study in the humanities—such as Freudian, Jungian, feminist, and cultural—may have social agendas based upon twentieth-century sensibilities, thus offering fewer insights into complexities characteristic of medieval situations. Structuralist or anthropological approaches, though, may contribute to new and more nuanced understandings of earlier texts and traditions. To be sure, if Kabbalists from different circles mingled and spread their knowledge in a significant manner, sociological tools are necessary.[2]

In order to broaden perspectives, it is insufficient to refer to other methods in sporadic and fragmentary ways; rather, by means of cooperation and dialogue, one should offer a more sustained and systematic treatment, as in the present book. The phenomenology of the different types of mystical experiences found in medieval and premodern literature can be understood in a more profound manner by referring to the results of experimental studies performed independently in the field of neurocognitive science. The more recent developments in this field, in theory, clinics, and brain-imaging technology, have been applied in this book in order to interpret Kabbalistic texts. This application corroborated the phenomenological categories extracted independently from the Kabbalistic literature. Moreover, the findings of neurocognitive mechanisms underlying specific mystical experiences may allow us to consider the possibility that central themes in the study of the human mind that draw the attention of modern philosophers and neuroscientists have already been reflected by the experiences of the prominent figures of Jewish mysticism under scrutiny in this book. A subdivision of natural studies, this approach is also relatively free of sociological and cultural influences, aiming to address cognitive brain-based mechanisms, which are relatively similar across societies and cultures. Finally, such an approach might have an explanatory value for other forms of visionary and mystical experiences present in texts from other mystical literature.

Nevertheless, no single methodology can facilitate a comprehensive understanding of the diversity of the vast

Kabbalistic literature, for it cannot reflect the diversity of any massive body of human creativity produced over a long period in diverse religious and social circumstances. Instead, we should better opt for an eclectic approach, better known as "the tool-box," or for what may be called perspectivism, which allows changing the methodological perspective in accordance with the specificity of the topics addressed by parts of the literature under scrutiny. Any attempt to impose a single methodological approach is prone to become an ideology that reduces the richness of the thought and practice of the Jewish mystics to simple "truths." There is no need to adopt any of the abovementioned methods as generating final truths since they are provisional and often feeble tools to be used carefully, wisely, and selectively; they are not truths to be indiscriminately projected onto too many texts and used to unconditionally generalize about the alleged homogenous nature of Kabbalah.

A difficult question is to what extent modern approaches in humanities that developed centuries after the analyzed materials were formulated can indeed help to clarify texts generated by cultures and circumstances that differ profoundly from those that hosted the modern thinkers. The application of such approaches is based on many implicit assumptions, especially one that sees in those approaches some form of scientific truth that does not depend on time and place or shifting circumstances. The systematic application of one of those approaches on a wide series of texts written by different authors, often separated by centuries and continents, might be challenging. The problems are obvious: whether sociological, psychological, phenomenological, or theological, those approaches are hardly unified, and divergences among the various psychological approaches are evident. If a Freudian approach is accepted, what about the Jungian one? If a theological approach is adopted, how is it that so many books on the theology of the Hebrew Bible do not agree with each other? This is the reason why we see a massive subscription to one single approach, a reduction of a complex corpus of thought to a limited number of ideas, injected by the scholar anachronistically into the interpreted texts.

Nevertheless, it is hard to avoid the pertinence of those approaches, formulated by intellectual prodigies, especially since they turned into conceptual tools that are part of the quotidian language, part of the transformation of information in communication. This is the reason why we subscribe to the "toolbox" approach, giving limited emphasis to any one approach, without rejecting any of them. Here, we adopt a neurocognitive approach in order to analyze a limited set of Kabbalistic texts belonging to ecstatic Kabbalah, which are very far from identical with the vast Kabbalistic literature.[3] While we believe the findings and comparisons made in this book are based on a solid ground—the human neurocognitive system—we emphasize that this component, though strong, is only a part of the rich picture of the mystical experience.

2. Ecstatic Kabbalah as a Seminal Investigation of the Human Self

The phenomenologies of the Kabbalistic material analyzed in this book and their comparison to modern cognitive experiments in healthy people and to observations in neurological patients suggest that major trends in Jewish Kabbalah managed to alter distinct neurocognitive mechanisms through the use of specific techniques. These excitations caused a change in the mystic's processing of functions related to his own self, such as the sense of embodiment or visuo-spatial perspective taking, leading to different variants of autoscopic and trance experiences and accompanied by prominent prophetic-like experiences of a "speaking double" or internal "maggidic" voice, thus facilitating further expansion of the borders of the mind and consciousness. We therefore propose that it is the mystical technique that leads the mystic to experience autoscopy, heautoscopy, out-of-body experience, or trance. The mystic might interpret these as sacred or prophetic experiences that reveal mystical secrets about human or divine nature.

Since the introduction of neuroimaging, dozens of studies have investigated the so-called neural mechanism underlying mystical techniques, especially meditation, which best fits the neuroimaging theater. However, such a "brain-mapping" approach is limited and different from ours. Here, we did not scan practitioners from certain traditions using functional MRI or electrical neuroimaging during their mystical exercises or attempts. Rather, we tried to stress the importance of the assemblage of technical, sociocultural, and linguistic factors for the construction of the human self, as based on physiological and neurocognitive characteristics that were altered by the use of ecstatic mystical techniques.

Adapting phenomenological, neurological, and neuro-cognitive approaches, we have suggested how major trends in Jewish mysticism helped mystics to achieve their mystical experiences by using practical techniques that affected their "intrinsic" self-processing and sense of embodiment. These techniques activate brain mechanisms at the temporo-parietal/ precuneal, medial-temporal, or medial prefrontal/orbito-frontal cortices, which together form the "intrinsic" system governing the processing of body and self.[4] Such an approach presents a valuable benefit to consciousness studies and to the neuropsychological understanding of the "self" since it separates the "self" from the body on different levels. We may now extend the proposal presented in the introduction of this book which stated that contemporary folk-psychology about the mind might have emerged from the older notion of the "soul" or "proto-concept of mind," and we hope that the reader is now convinced that the ecstatic Kabbalah mystics indeed used exstatic autoscopic and dissociative phenomena as early and pioneering experimental models in the investigation of the philosophy of mind and the cognition of the human "self." While our technology has advanced much since the time of ecstatic Kabbalah, our ability for introspection has not. Just as our cultural and scientific lives may be influenced by masterpieces in literature or art, similar inspiration may also derive from the philosophical, psychological, and cognitive work of early scholars, such as the Jewish mystics described in this book. Their call for the reader to look at the self from a nonhabitual perspective, and from this perspective to further introspect, still holds as much as it did centuries ago, and maybe even more.

Appendix A

The External and Internal Worlds: Functional Networks in the Human Brain

1. Large-Scale Networks in the Human Brain: Function and Anatomy

The human brain, an aggregation of neurons and supporting cells, receives and interprets an immense array of sensory information, controls a variety of motor behaviors, governs the body, and manages high cognitive functions. It makes complex decisions, thinks creatively, feels emotions, recognizes different forms and patterns, generalizes, and differentiates. Moreover, it can carry out all these tasks in a nearly simultaneous manner.[1] Although the brain contains many other important parts, such as the cerebellum, brainstem, and basal ganglia, we focus here on the cerebral cortex, which is a major substrate for functions that convey comprehension, cognition, and communication (Figure 7). More specifically, we consider the different cortical regions as the building blocks of the functional cognitive brain. The

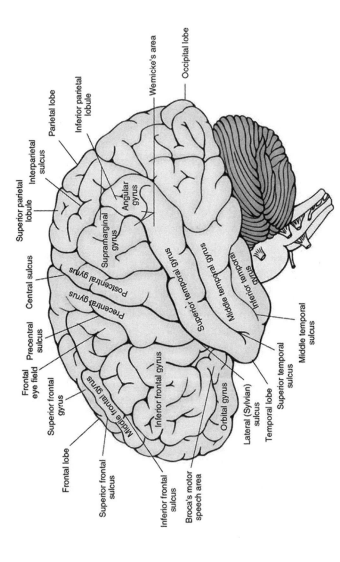

Figure 7. The main divisions of the central nervous system. The cerebral cortex with its four lobes (frontal, temporal, parietal, occipital), the subcortical nuclei, the cerebellum, and the brainstem are shown (from http://what-when-how.com/neuroscience/overview-of-the-central-nervous-system-gross-anatomy-of-the-brain-part-1/).

largest area of the cerebral cortex is the neocortex, which is the top layer of the cerebral hemispheres, mostly involved in functions such as sensory perception, generation of motor commands, spatial navigation, memory, language, reasoning, and conscious thought. Following Marsel M. Mesulam's seminal work, the neocortex may be subdivided into two major zones: the unimodal (modality specific) and heteromodal (integrates across modalities) cortices.[2] Unimodal sensory cortices are constituted by neurons that mostly respond to stimulation in only one sensory modality. Sensory organs—such as the eyes, ears, and different receptors all over the body—project information regarding the external world to the primary sensory cortices (including the primary visual, auditory, and somatosensory cortices). The information is then processed by unimodal association areas, which treat one specific modality of information (although new evidence suggests that these regions might also share multisensory information with other modalities). This input is further processed in heteromodal cortices. The heteromodal cortices are not confined to any single sensory modality but receive input from different unimodal areas and integrate the information to one coherent percept. Thus, for instance, the visual recognition ("what") system may identify an object or face, and the visual spatial ("where") system can localize it; a language area can then identify this object or face in a linguistic pattern and name it. These heteromodal cortices are mostly located at the posterior parietal, prefrontal, and lateral temporal parts of the brain (Figure 8).[3]

For a specific sensory or motor task to be performed, the joint work of different unimodal and heteromodal cortices is required. Higher heteromodal regions in the posterior parietal, lateral, and medial temporal and prefrontal cortices as well as in the hippocampus and the amygdala link distributed informa-

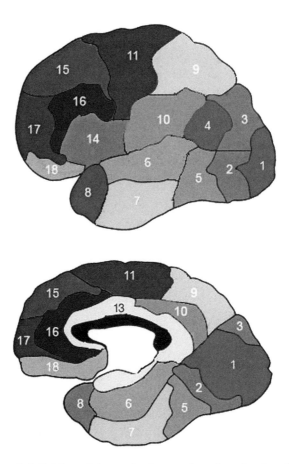

Figure 8. Subdivision of the cerebral cortex into functional regions, shown from lateral (top) and medial (bottom) views. Regions in the primary and (relatively) unimodal cortex include the visual cortex (1–3), primary auditory cortex (6, 7) the primary sensorimotor cortices (9, anterior part), and the language regions of Broca (14) and Wernicke (6). Heteromodal regions include the angular gyrus (4), the lateral occipito-temporal complex (5), the temporal pole (8), the posterior parietal cortex (9), the temporo-parietal junction (10), the limbic/para-limbic system and the insula (12 [not visible], 13), and regions in the frontal (11, 15–17) and prefrontal cortices (18). Division to functional Brodmann areas (fBAs) as used in S. Arzy, Y. Arzouan et al., "The 'intrinsic' system in the human cortex and self-projection: a data driven analysis." *Neuroreport* 21 (2010): 569–74.

tion into coherent multimodal assemblies ("network of networks") necessary for spatial navigation, attention, object recognition, execution of action, memory, and emotion by coactivating cortical large-scale networks among distributed brain areas. These large-scale networks connect the activated brain regions within the network, facilitating parallel processing and multidirectional approaches that enable the network to solve complicated tasks in a very short time. Individual cortical areas might dynamically shift among networks depending on the task's requirements. This functional plasticity allows a rapid association and dissociation of local clusters into distinct functional subgroups, depending on the network that recruits them. A distinct advantage of this mechanism is that it dynamically creates a context for the local information expressed in each area of the network by interactions with other areas.[4]

Mesulam identified five large-scale networks in the human brain (Figure 9); new networks studies have extended our understanding of the brain's network organization.[5]

1. Spatial attention and corporeal awareness network. The parietal lobe, especially in the right hemisphere, is conventionally said to be specialized for spatial cognition (one's behavior as an agent in space). This relies on the role of the parietal lobe in integrating information from the different senses in the manipulation of objects and in visuo-spatial processing. The parietal lobe constructs maps of one's own body as well as of the spaces near to and far from the body. Parietal-lobe–based neurocognitive mechanisms locate oneself on these different maps with respect to other subjects or objects. In addition, these

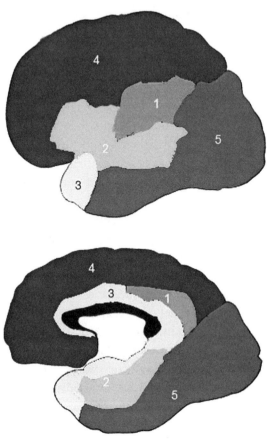

Figure 9. The five major functional large-scale networks of the human brain (as described by M. M. Mesulam), shown from lateral (top) and medial (bottom) views: 1, spatial attention and corporeal awareness network; 2, language network; 3, memory-emotion network; 4, executive function–comportment network; and 5, face and object identification network.

mechanisms are involved in distinguishing the self from its surroundings and in representing other people with respect to one's self. Notably, not only the parietal lobe but also the hippocampus plays a central role in spatial processing and navigation.[6]

2. Language network. Language allows individuals to connect to each other and thus to create a society. Even on the individual level, thoughts are formulated in words and sentences. This fundamental component of our mental world depends mostly on two distinguished brain regions in the left hemisphere: Broca's and Wernicke's areas. Broca's area in the frontal lobe is responsible for the articulation and synthesis of speech, and Wernicke's area, around the posterior superior temporal region, is responsible for language comprehension. Regions in the right hemisphere also contribute to linguistic aspects such as prosody and intonation. Left posterior parietal regions manage reading and writing. Taken together, this network of networks gives rise to our linguistic ability.

3. Memory-emotion network. Here the hippocampus and the amygdala play key roles. Different types of memories are stored in different parts of the cortex. Autobiographical memories, closely related to emotions, are first laid in the hippocampus and then in distributed brain regions, like the posterior frontal and inferior parietal cortices. Memories that are important for procedural-motor activities are laid in the executive and motor (frontal and prefrontal) cortices.[7]

Semantic memories are supposed to be stored in
the anterior temporal lobe, adjacent to the hippocampus. The amygdala, which lies in front of
the hippocampus, plays a key role in the processing of emotions. The emotional content of different memories is processed in the amygdala,
and, consequently, when memory is retrieved,
this adjacent brain structure weighs it according
to its emotional impact.

4. Executive function–comportment network. This
   includes frontal and posterior parietal areas.
   Frontal areas receive information from posterior
   ones and then cooperate with the motor cortices
   to execute an action. Fronto-parietal activity is
   thus crucial for essential brain functions such as
   attention, working memory, autobiographical
   memory retrieval, and conscious visual perception.[8] The frontal lobe serves as an executive part
   of the cortex for higher-order functions, including reasoning and abstraction; planning and
   initiation of activity; monitoring and shaping of
   behavior, including inhibition of maladaptive
   behavior; problem solving; and coordination of
   motor and sensory functions into a coherent and
   goal-directed stream of behavior.

5. What-where-who network (faces, bodies, and
   objects identification). Visual information coming
   from the primary visual cortex in the occipital lobe
   is processed in two interconnected yet dissociated
   visual pathways: a "ventral" pathway, which extends into the temporal lobe and is thought to be
   primarily involved in visual object recognition

("what" system), and a "dorsal" pathway, which extends into the parietal lobes and is thought to be more involved in extracting information about "where" an object is located or "how" to execute visually guided actions toward it ("where" system). Specifically, subregions in the "what" system are specialized in processing faces, human bodies, or body parts and other certain objects or patterns.[9]

These networks are organized in the brain such that the more frontal regions are responsible for executive and motor activities, while posterior regions are involved in the perception and processing of different sensory input. Medial temporal structures are involved in more "internal" functions such as memory and emotions.

Some Principles in Functional Neuroanatomy

Prefrontal Cortex

The prefrontal cortex is an extensive heteromodal cortex, largely responsible for the execution of behavior. Lesions in the orbito-frontal cortex distort the integration of personality into specific compartmental patterns and strategies of thinking as well as the inhibition of inappropriate desires and urges. This is ex-emplified in the famous case of Phineas Gage, who had a complete change in personality after suffering extensive damage to his prefrontal cortex. The prefrontal cortex has a high density of interconnections with almost all integrating areas in the cerebral cortex and through these might activate or suppress different networks. It is probably by these connections that the prefrontal cortex inhibits impulses that are not appropriate to the general comportment designated by the cerebral cortex at a given time and circumstance. This way, a system's output can always be inhibited and its influence on conscious states and voluntary behavior reduced or eliminated. The medial prefrontal cortex might be necessary for self-referential mental activity, regarding "simulating" or "rehearsing" future behavior. The prefrontal cortex is also responsible for binding thoughts, memories, and experiences with appropriate visceral and bodily states; damage to these areas can interfere with the interaction between behavior and visceral reactions. Finally, the dorsolateral part of the prefrontal cortex is responsible for planning and execution of actions and for working memory, a function that enables mental manipulation and online retention of information.[10]

Parietal Cortex

The parietal lobe is divided into two major parts: the more anterior somatosensory cortex and the posterior parietal cortex. The posterior parietal cortex is situated at the intersection of visual, auditory, and tactile cortices, functioning as the "crossroads of the brain." The posterior parietal cortex is not only located at the junction of multiple sensory regions, but also projects to several cortical and subcortical areas and is engaged in a host of cognitive operations, including spatial representation and updating, attention, coordinate transformation, and abstract motor planning; a specialized region within the parietal lobe, the inferior parietal lobule, processes self-related activities such as agency, self-other discrimination, visual perspective taking, and perception of whole bodies.[11]

Patients suffering from lesions at their right posterior parietal cortex demonstrate problems in performing various spatial skills, including navigation and topographical orientation (though this is managed in the medial part of the parietal cortex, the precuneus), or even with copying a simple construction or drawing a simple form (constructional apraxia). Such patients might also manifest spatial neglect syndrome, ignoring things on their left-hand side.[12] Patients with right posterior parietal lesions may also suffer from body perception disorders such as asomatognosia (an unawareness of one's own body or body parts), somatoparaphrenia (denial of ownership of a body part), or anosognosia (unawareness of illness).[13]

Medial Temporal Lobe

The medial temporal lobe includes a system of anatomically related structures that are essential for memory functions and emotions. The hippocampus and adjacent regions work in harmony with the neocortex to establish and maintain long-term memory; ultimately, through a process of consolidation, long-term memories are stored in the neocortex. An adjacent region, the amygdala, is critically involved in the formation and storage of lasting memories of emotional experiences.[14]

Episodic memory of life events allows humans to construct a unique record of experience and knowledge based on their own life experiences as well as lives of others. Episodic memories need to be incorporated into a coherent context (or "story") through a binding function, passing through a gateway in the hippocampus for encoding and then retrieval although they are not necessarily stored there. Facts and events are initially coded at multiple sites. The hippocampal gateway enables the appropriate coding of events as memories as well as further organization and retrieval, which coherently stores and reactivates distributed information.[15] The hippocampus receives input from numerous heteromodal and unimodal association areas of all sensorial modalities. In the other direction, as additional linkages become established through reciprocal connections among unimodal and heteromodal areas, the relevant information becomes less dependent on the function of the hippocampus and adjacent regions and can be accessed directly through the activation of cortical regions. The transitional period between the hippocampal and cortical storage of memories allows new memories to enter associative readjustments before being assimilated in a more permanent form.[16] Moreover, during encoding or retrieval, memories are continuously further modified ("re-biography"). In accessing knowledge of characteristics of subjects or objects, recall is based on stable associations of episodes consolidated throughout life and distributed to be stored in the neocortex.[17] The interconnections with the amygdala and the limbic system emphasize the emotional load of self-referenced autobiographical memories.[18]

Finally, medial temporal structures, especially the insular cortex, are extensively interconnected with the hypothalamus, which through neural and neuron-hormonal mechanisms controls the internal milieu of the body. These range from the most fundamental processes, such as autonomic tonus, electrolyte balance, body temperature, and sexual phases, to the experience and expression of emotions. In keeping these hypothalamic functions, medial temporal structures serve as cortical regulators for these fundamental functions of body systems.[19]

Laterality

Anatomically, the two cerebral hemispheres are almost identical. Also functionally, the "primary" cortical zones, where visual, auditory, or somatosensory information is projected on the cortex, are supposed to be symmetrical. We know, however,

from everyday life, that most of us are right handed. Considering
the contralateral connection between limbs and hemispheres, it
might be assumed that the left hemisphere is more dominant in
the control of skilled movements.[20] The left hemisphere is also
more active in linguistic tasks since it contains the abovementioned
areas of Broca (language production) and Wernicke (language
comprehension). In contrast, the right hemisphere is important
in spatial cognition and in distributed attention to the extrapersonal space and in spatial attention and navigation, agency, mental imagery, drawing or managing objects, own-body perception,
and visuo-spatial perspective taking. The right hemisphere is also
specialized among others in coordinating emotional expression
and experience, together with the amygdala and other structures
of the limbic system.[21] This functional "division of labor" (though
somehow challenged by recent studies) is also supported by evidence from lesion studies that show different faculties to be
impaired after unilateral damage (e.g., damage to certain association cortices in the left hemisphere produces language disorders,
whereas damage to parts in the right hemisphere produces spatial
cognition disorders); functional neuroimaging studies also show
differential patterns of activation between the two hemispheres
for these and other functions. This asymmetry appears at the
level of the heteromodal association cortex. Therefore, cortical
regions showing asymmetry are mostly found in the prefrontal
cortex and in regions located around the junction of the occipital,
temporal, and parietal lobes.[22]

2. The External and Internal Worlds

Classical approaches saw the brain as a computer, processing input in a hierarchical fashion and then producing an
output.[23] However, new data indicate that the brain does not

act only in this "ascending" hierarchical manner, in which "higher" centers are activated later and contain more abstract information than "lower" regions, but that it is also active in a "descending" manner, in which higher regions modify the lower region activity.[24] Indeed, many aspects of cognition and behavior are not stimulus-driven rather but are influenced by internally driven cognitive processes, action schemas, emotions, or memories processed in cortical (and subcortical) networks, which together create the so-called default mode network of brain activity.[25] The default-mode network, encompassing mostly the posterior parietal (the cuneus/precuneus medially and the temporo-parietal junction laterally) and the medial prefrontal cortices, is a main network active during rest when no external stimulus is delivered. This network manages memories, future thinking, mind wandering, imagination, and other processes related to the experiential and mental life. Interestingly, this activity is much more extensive than those related to the external world, as reflected by comparison of the energy consumed by the brain during extrinsic and intrinsic activities. Not only the default-mode network is active in rest. Sensorimotor simulations of the external world are in fact widely implicated in human cognition. In mental imagery, for instance, one might simulate visual, auditory, or kinesthetic manifestations without actually experiencing them. This imagery involves analogous representations of different aspects of the external world not currently perceived. Thus, for instance, while speech is being imagined, a wide range of lexical regions in the brain are activated, even without speech perception or production.[26] The "mirror neuron" system, which reflects other people's activities but activates motor systems related to these activities in the observer as if performed by this observer, is another important domain in which imagery activates the brain as acting with no activity really occurring.[27] Another important source of perceptions and processing not emanating from the external world is the "internal milieu," namely, the body, which designs our conscious or mental state. Thus, when we are stressed, different stimuli will be perceived as stressful, for different hormones secreted in stress have a further influence on the brain. Taken together, these lines of evidence demonstrate how perception is influenced not only by the external world, but also by the internal milieu and by different mental states, actions, and comportments (Figure 10).[28]

The mutual influences of the external world and the "internal milieu" on information processing in the brain might be regarded as bottom-up and top-down processing, respectively. Bottom-up activity is the common basis of perception: a stimulus is perceived by sense organs, passed to the primary cortex, then to different levels of the associative cortex, and finally to higher heteromodal cortices. Top-down processing is determined by the endogenous state in different brain regions before stimulus perception, by expectancy, emotion, and attention.[29] Top-down resources allow the brain to create predictions about the forthcoming stimuli and influence them accordingly. This means that both the external sensory input and the internal knowledge are crucial for perception. Accordingly, recent studies also point to the subdivision of the cerebral cortex into two main functional networks: one is related mostly to processing of external input ("extrinsic" system), and another is mostly dedicated to processing the "internal milieu" ("intrinsic" system).[30]

To summarize, external input is perceived in the human brain by the sensory system. The visual, auditory, and somatosensory systems supply the major channels of communication with the external world, together with vestibular, gustatory, and

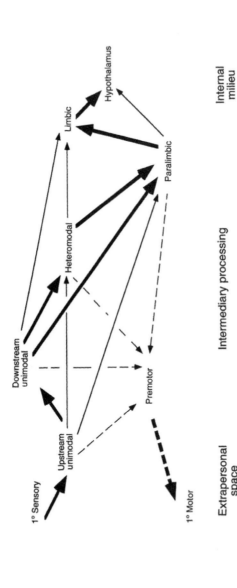

Figure 10. The brain as a bridge between the external and internal worlds. The primary and heteromodal cortex and the limbic systems are shown, according to their relation to the external world (extrapersonal space), intermediary processing, and the internal milieu. Solid arrows illustrate direct sensory neural connections in the visual and auditory modalities; thick arrows represent more massive connections than thin arrows; dashed arrows illustrate motor output pathways (from M. M. Mesulam, "From sensation to cognition." *Brain* 121 [1998]: 1013–52, used by permission of Oxford University Press).

olfactory systems. Input from these channels is then integrated with internally generated states such as memories and emotions. The outcomes of this integration may be defined as consciousness, comportment, or cognition and include the diverse manifestations of memory, emotion, attention, planning, language, decision-making, judgment, and thought. This integrative processing enables identical stimuli to trigger different processes independent of context, past memories, and future needs. "Bottom-up" and "top-down" are heuristic terms for what is in reality a large-scale network that integrates both incoming and endogenous activity.[31] The next section reviews different proposals for how this integration is performed.

3. Integration of Information in the Brain

A property of consciousness is that it is a unified experience of the different perceptions from the external world and the internal states of the experiencer. Although different modules in the brain are responsible for processing the different aspects of what one is experiencing—such as color, shape, weight, sound, distance, spatiality, or movement—we perceive them all as unified characteristics of the experienced object or scene. This is known as the "binding problem."[32] Previous theories claimed that the hierarchical organization of the brain suggests associative areas that mediate between sensory and motor areas, providing the basis for integration.[33] Contemporary theories argue that networks of reciprocal interactions are the key for integration.[34] One proposal for such a theory considers cross-system interactions. Different neuroimaging and neurophysiological studies indicate that top-down influences originate in prefrontal and parietal cortices.[35] The cross-system theory suggests that high-order "transmodal" regions in the prefrontal and parietal cortices send signals to the more basic association areas and modify their activity accordingly. Transmodal areas are not centers for storing convergent knowledge but rather for integrating and accessing the relevant distributed information. These parietal and prefrontal signals are assumed to exert top-down control over routing the information flow in the brain. These higher order cortices can not only encode and store perceptual characteristics of an external event but are further specialized in specific processing and integration of information. In addition, during processing, the input is extensively filtered, while only the most relevant information is integrated.[36] Together with limbic and paralimbic regions, parietal and prefrontal cortices create the complex subjective experience of the external world and internal milieu.

Similarly, the "global workspace theory" emphasizes a two-way flow between conscious and unconscious activity.[37] It assumes that the brain is composed of different distributed networks, which are activated subconsciously. Some of them, primarily at the prefrontal cortex and parietal cortex, integrate, retain, and distribute coherent neuronal events that are reportable as conscious. Unconscious networks, emotions, and memories shape and support the conscious events. Another similar theory is "neuronal group selection," which proposes that signals derived from high-order regions "reenter" the lower levels of processing, creating a recursive loop of reciprocal connections.[38]

Models of synchronic oscillation and temporal binding are different from the abovementioned hierarchical theories yet are somehow complementary. These models assume that synchronic activity between different brain regions unifies them to a network that perceives and processes given input. This opinion is supported by findings of increased correlation between activities in different brain regions during multi-modal task execution.[39] Synchrony (communication through coherence) and temporal binding models claim that inputs acting in a temporally organized manner have a stronger mutual influence than in desynchronized processes. Moreover, a crucial component of these models is that synchrony can be internally induced by the brain. To be sure, in contrast to the hierarchical models that see more "abstract" regions as controlling basic association cortices, synchrony and temporal binding models depict a continuous influence on the network of the different synchronized regions. These latter models therefore predict that neurons which respond to the same stimulus object fire in a synchronous way.[40] This theory is supported by electrophysiological studies, which showed an enhancement of high-frequency brain oscillations in tasks that require attention, learning, emotion, or motivation.[41] This "coherence" between brain regions was found especially between parietal and prefrontal regions, in particular while activity was modulated by top-down processes. Moreover, changes were observed in these regions even in the absence of external stimuli (such as during mental imagery), reflecting the important role of synchrony and binding in governing intrinsic activity.[42]

To summarize, the above reviewed theories endeavor to explain how spatiotemporally distinguished brain activities join to create one coherent functional process. This processing is influenced not only by directly related external stimuli and associated processing, but also by cross-modal influences from other sensory modalities, memories, or emotions and by the "internal milieu." Integration of information seems to be implemented by large-scale networks of prefrontal, parietal, and medial temporal areas. Top-down activities could then be mediated by the entraining effects that such networks, carrying a high level of information, might exert on networks processing new information. From an electrophysiological point-of-view, coherent synchronized brain oscillation might bind different activities together into harmonized processing. Notably, all these theories encompassing the large-scale level cannot encompass the whole computational picture, and much more detailed work is needed in order to better understand information processing in the brain.

4. Embodiment, Subjectivity, and Integration

It has become more and more accepted that the human mind should be understood in the context of its relations with the body and the surrounding environment, for the mind's carrier—namely, the human brain—evolved primarily for sensorial and motor activities, performed through the body upon the surrounding environment.[43] This notion has its roots in the works of the father of modern psychology, William James, or later in James J. Gibson's "ecological psychology."[44] These theories notice that the brain, the body, and the environment are highly structured dynamical systems, coupled to one another on multiple levels, thus combining to mutually embedded systems, in which neuronal (brain), somatic (body), and environmental elements are likely to interact to produce global-organism environment processes, which in turn affect their constituent elements.[45] Gregory Bateson's theory of "ecology of mind" sees the human self as an "aggregate of habits of perception and adaptive actions plus, from moment to moment, our immanent states of action."[46] The human self, according to Bateson, is a feed-forward system of perceptions and actions. This self-model is further influenced by urges, forces, feelings, and other emotions.

Recent findings in cognitive neuroscience support these theories. With respect to the body, it has been suggested that human existence in a singular body binds consciousness together. Moreover, actions and perceptions are also affected by the body since bodily and emotional states influence one's perception of—and action in—the external world. Action and perception might thus be regarded as premeditated by the internal milieu, body states, and the environment.[47]

With regard to the environment, the organism senses a function of how it moves in the environment and how it acts upon it. Indeed, the cognitive system is mostly concentrated on inputs and outputs relevant to the performed activity. For example, the substantial role of vision is not to build rich inner models of the surrounding reality, but rather to use visual information to act upon the environment in order to improve one's survival. The environment thus not only supplies the perceived stimuli, but also designs the way in which they are perceived.[48]

It is proposed that prefrontal and parietal cortices play a key role in creating this brain-body-world interphase. This is also reflected by the role of these regions in the abovementioned default-mode network and processing of self-related information.[49] This notion is further supported by studies of people in unconscious states (deep sleep, general anesthesia, vegetative state, and epileptic loss of consciousness) which found that coherent activity at the prefrontal and parietal cortex appears during anesthesia and deep sleep but is enhanced in wakefulness. Accordingly, transcranial magnetic stimulation (TMS) applied during deep sleep induced a decline of connectivity between different brain regions, but not the fronto-parietal cortex.[50] This might suggest that consciousness is dependent on cooperative processes in a highly distributed network governed by the prefrontal and parietal cortices.

5. Conclusion

The cerebral cortex establishes consciousness and cognition by interactively perceiving and integrating functions that combine information from a multitude of sources. This includes not only various external perceptions but also internally generated information representing intentional and unintentional imaginations, past memories and future predictions, emotions, plans, and bodily states.[51] Information from the external world is perceived by sensory organs and projected onto the primary sensorial areas. It is next processed in unimodal specific areas and then in heteromodal association areas. Simultaneously, actions, bodily states, previous experiences, and patterns affect this process, which provides the neural bridge that mediates between the external world and the "internal milieu." This process further enables the associative elaboration of sensory information, its translation into motor actions, and the integration of different experiences with emotions and motivations. In the integration of processing across different brain regions; between body, brain, and environment; and from subconscious to conscious processing, the prefrontal, medial-frontal, and parietal cortices seem to play a central role. Their mutual activity, together with other unimodal and heteromodal mechanisms intercorrelated via a variety of brain rhythms, finally gives rise to a behaving, perceiving, reacting, and reflecting human self.

Appendix B
Abraham Abulafia the Mystic and His Theory and Technique

Abraham ben Shmuel Abulafia (1240–ca. 1291) was born in Saragossa, in the Basque region, and lived in Tudela until the age of twenty. In 1260 he left Spain to search for the legendary river of Sambatyon and arrived in Acre, in the lower Galilee. He then returned to Greece, where he married, and traveled to Italy, where he started his studies in philosophy, especially of Maimonides's *Guide for the Perplexed*, in Capua with Rabbi Hillel of Verona early in the 1260s. Toward the end of the decade Abulafia returned to Spain and started his interest in Kabbalah in Barcelona in 1270, when he also had a revelation presumably regarding his messianic mission. After some time in Castile, where he taught the *Guide for the Perplexed* in accordance with his Kabbalistic understanding, he left Spain around 1273 for the Byzantine Empire, where he remained until 1279, staying especially in the city of Patras. At the beginning of that year Abulafia had a series of revelations that strengthened the earlier one and encouraged him to try to

meet the pope. He returned to Italy and taught during 1279–1280
in Capua and traveled to Soriano nel Cimino, north of Rome,
to meet the pope in the summer of 1280. However, the pope
died before Abulafia's arrival. After being arrested and impris-
oned for two weeks in Rome, Abulafia left for Sicily, where he
spent most of the decade in Messina, teaching several students.
He also had students in Palermo. Between 1279 and 1291 he
composed most of his writings, in which he intensified his
messianic propaganda and claimed that he was both a prophet
and a messiah. As a result of such claims he was criticized by
the foremost legalistic authority of Sephardic Jewry of the time,
Rabbi Shlomo ben Abraham ibn Aderet; after a fierce controversy between the two men, Abulafia was banned from Spanish
schools, leading to a rejection of his teachings in the Iberian
Peninsula. He wrote his last dated book in 1291; we do not know
when and where he died. He wrote several dozen books, most
of which survived in manuscript form and have been printed
for the first time only since 2000.

Abulafia designated his form of Kabbalah as the Kabbalah of divine names and prophetic Kabbalah, that is, ecstatic
Kabbalah, in order to distinguish it from sefirotic Kabbalah,
which developed in southern France and northern Spain for a
century before Abulafia's Kabbalah. An analysis of the phenomenological structure of ecstatic Kabbalah when compared with
its Spanish counterparts may help us to see it in an appropriate
light. Its emphasis on the centrality of mystical experiences,
including revelations; on lengthy discussions on anomian mystical techniques, namely on practices differing from traditional Jewish rituals; on Abulafia's specific eschatological
attitudes; as well as its individualistic and at the same time
universalist approach diverge drastically from the spiritual
character of the Spanish Kabbalists. The sources of these

characteristics include Abulafia's idiosyncratic personality and the esoteric material that inspired him, especially Maimonides's *Guide* and a variety of philosophical writings translated from Arabic into Hebrew. Abulafia differs from the vast majority of his contemporary Kabbalists. In addition, his studies of commentaries on *Sefer Yetzirah*, especially those dealing with letter permutations, supplied major components for the linguistic propensities of his form of Kabbalah.

Abulafia's detailed quest for ecstasy by means of his techniques, in his term *nevu'ah* (prophecy), is part of a broader quest that was inherent in Jewish mysticism outside of the Iberian Peninsula. This is evident especially in the Ashkenazic provinces, that is, Germany and northern France, where a variety of figures were designated as prophets during the first part of the thirteenth century. In the writings of Ashkenazic authors it is possible to discern some of the features of Abulafia's techniques to reach ecstasy, especially the specific types of letter combinations and their vocalizations. Thus a unique combination of two quite conceptual types of religion—the philosophical and the linguistic, which played only a negligible role in other forms of Kabbalah—is important for the spiritual character of Abulafia's Kabbalah. His mystical experiences include a variety of phenomena, such as prophecy, which has strong autoscopic features, and mystical union, envisioned as a noetic conjunction of the human and cosmic intellects.

Even a superficial perusal of Abulafia's vast Kabbalistic literature shows that quasi-gnostic mythologoumena and symbols, characteristic of theosophical Kabbalah, were as far from his worldview as they were from that of medieval Jewish philosophers. The inner path, which emphasizes more the transformation of the human psyche, or "intellect" in Abulafia's nomenclature, tends to minimize, intrinsically, the relevance of the inner divine structure that characterizes theosophical Kabbalah. Likewise, the theurgical understanding of the role of the commandments is absent in his writings. Symbolism, at least in the manner it was defined by scholars of Kabbalah, is also irrelevant for Abulafia's Kabbalah. In lieu of the centrality of nomian practices, the magical-mystical status of the Hebrew language and its components come to the fore. Thus, the sweeping definitions of Kabbalah in general fail to do justice to one important trend in Jewish mysticism: ecstatic Kabbalah.

What does such a split in the history of Jewish mysticism imply? First and foremost, it shows that the mystical and technical elements in the various phases of Jewish mysticism are not disparate, unrelated phenomena; on the contrary, beyond the terminological and sometimes conceptual divergences between the various schools in Jewish mysticism, there is also a substantial element of continuity: during the High Middle Ages the *Heikhalot* literature was still inspiring forms of mystical practices, and it deeply influenced the Hasidei Ashkenaz. Their concerns with magical and mystical techniques did not vanish with the disappearance of their group; the reverberations of their hermeneutics, their mystical techniques, and maybe even their ideals of mystical experience are still discernible in the second half of the thirteenth century. Ecstatic Kabbalah has absorbed elements of these two schools into a wider system, deeply informed by Maimonidean theology, and offered to the Jewish mystics of later generations, especially to Rabbi Moshe Cordovero and his form of Kabbalah, an alternative to the Spanish theurgical-theosophical Kabbalah. Hasidism, deeply affected by Safedian Kabbalah and its offspring, and apparently also by other direct and indirect contacts with ecstatic Kabbalah, elaborated several forms of mystical practices that are reminiscent of ecstatic Kabbalah.

Therefore, the ecstatic element in Jewish mysticism should be understood as an important constant of varying intensity, rather than as the prerogative of a certain phase or school. The emphasis on ecstatic experience does not exhaust the differences between the main target of ecstatic Kabbalah and Zoharic Kabbalah. In fact, ecstasy is deeply related, in both ecstatic Kabbalah and East European Hasidism, to some other important spiritual features that may help us to articulate a more adequate understanding of the nature of Jewish mysticism in general. As we have seen, modern scholars have generically described this lore as symbolic, mythical, and gnostic, without mentioning that these characteristics, even if were they appropriate for the main trend of Kabbalah, are not relevant, or are marginal, to ecstatic Kabbalah. In my opinion, this is the case also for Hasidism.

The fact that Abulafia influenced Jewish figures outside of Spain, especially in the Byzantine Empire, Italy, Sicily, and the land of Israel, demonstrates that the geographical characterization of his form of Kabbalah as Spanish, such as Gershom Scholem defined it, fails to take into account the basic historical facts as we know them. A person born in Spain does not necessarily generate a "Spanish Kabbalah."

The stark divergences between the variety of Kabbalistic schools and Abulafia's Kabbalah were already recognized as early as the 1280s by Abraham Abulafia himself, who spoke about his Kabbalah as a prophetic Kabbalah, as against the inferior, sefirotic one. In slightly different forms, this distinction was repeated by two Christian Kabbalists, Giovanni Pico della Mirandola and Johannes Reuchlin. Surprisingly, Scholem, who himself accepted this distinction, attributed it to Reuchlin. It is therefore not the insight of modern scholarship that there were two major and divergent trends in Kabbalah, and it is regrettable that some modern scholars disregard the obvious source of this distinction in the self-understanding of the early Kabbalists and attempt to reduce the phenomenological gap between the two trends.

Obviously, the discussions in this book offer neurocognitive explanations for only a few of the various forms of mystical experiences of ecstatic Kabbalah. Other forms, such as the vision of letters enlarging during the experience (macropsia), or taking on colors (synesthesia), as described by Abulafia, are not explained here in the framework of autoscopic experiences. Moreover, many other forms of experience found in Kabbalistic literature in general, several of which may also have a distinct neurocognitive basis, are not addressed here. Our efforts therefore have not been directed toward one single explanation that reduces the variety of experiences to one single neurocognitive model. Further research may explain and extend the variety of experiences, using these and other models, within and outside of the neurocognitive sciences.

Notes

Introduction

1. Arzy, Idel et al., "Speaking with One's Self"; Idel, *Kabbalah*; Bourguignon, *Possession*; Hollenback, *Mysticism*; de Souzenelle, *Le symbolisme du corps humain*; Forman, "What Does Mysticism Have to Teach Us?"
2. Idel, *The Mystical Experience in Abraham Abulafia*; Idel, *Kabbalah*; Forman, "What Does Mysticism Have to Teach Us?"
3. Idel, *Kabbalah*; Arzy, Idel et al., "Speaking with One's Self."
4. Metzinger, "The Pre-Scientific Concept of a 'Soul,'" p. 1.

1
Justification of a Neurocognitive Approach to Mystical Experiences

1. Liebes, "Kivunim Hadashim Be-Heker Ha-Kabbalah."
2. Idel, "On the Theologization of Kabbalah"; Magid, "Gershom Scholem's Ambivalence"; Idel, "Some Remarks."
3. Most of the mystics for whom we have documents and all of the mystics dealt with in this book are men, although the discussed material may hold for women and men equally. For simplicity, the masculine pronoun forms will be used in this book.
4. Durkheim, *Elementary Forms*.

5. Forman, "What Does Mysticism Have to Teach Us?"; Smith, *Experience and God*.

6. Arzy, Idel et al., "Speaking with One's Self"; Hadot, "Exercices spirituels"; Hadot, *Qu'est-ce que la philosophie antique?*; Merlan, *Monopsychism, Mysticism, Metaconsciousness*; Moore, "Mystical Experience"; Morgan, *Platonic Piety*; Wallis, "Nous as Experience."

7. Arzy, Idel et al., "Speaking with One's Self"; Idel, *Language, Torah, and Hermeneutics*; Idel, *Kabbalah*.

8. Arzy, Idel et al., "Why Revelations Have Occurred on Mountains."

9. Idel, *Ascensions on High*; Idel, *The Mystical Experience in Abraham Abulafia*.

10. Arzy, Idel et al., "Speaking with One's Self"; Idel, *Language, Torah, and Hermeneutics*; Idel, *The Mystical Experience in Abraham Abulafia*.

11. Idel, *Ascensions on High*; Idel, *Hasidism*.

12. Gruenwald, "From Talmudic to Zoharic Homiletics."

13. Idel, *Kabbalah*; Idel, *Natan Ben Sa'adyah Har'ar (Sha'arei Tzedeq)*; Lewis, *Our Experience of God*.

14. Pike, *Mystic Union*.

15. Weber, *Ancient Judaism*.

16. Newberg, *Principles of Neuroethology*; Miller, *Oxford Handbook*; Lawson and McCauley, Rethinking Religion.

17. Burkert, *Homo Necans*.

18. Idel, "Between Rabbinism and Kabbalism."

2
Approaching Ecstatic Experiences

1. Buber, *Ecstatic Confessions*, p. 4.

2. Eliade, *Zalmoxis*; Eliade, *The Two and the One*; Eliade, *The Quest*; Eliade, *Yoga, Immortality and Freedom*; Eliade, *Rites and Symbols of Initiation*; Eliade, *Shamanism*; Eliade, *Myths, Dreams, and Mysteries*; Sullivan, *Icanchu's Drum*; Garb, *Shamanic Trance in Modern Kabbalah*.

3. Eliade, *Shamanism*; Eliade, *Myths, Dreams, and Mysteries*.

4. Hollenback, *Mysticism*, pp. 136–37.

5. Hellner-Eshed, "A River Issues Forth from Eden"; Idel, *Hasidism*; Idel, *The Mystical Experience in Abraham Abulafia*; Idel, *Kabbalah*; Idel, "On the Meanings of the Term 'Kabbalah' "; Wolfson, *Abraham Abulafia*; Bastide, *The Mystical Life*.

6. Idel, "On Some Forms of Order in Kabbalah."

7. Scholem, *Origins of the Kabbalah*, p. 55.

8. Ibid., pp. 122–23.

9. Ibid.; Ben Shlomo, "Gershom Scholem on Pantheism in the Kabbalah"; Scholem, *Major Trends in Jewish Mysticism*; Idel, "On the Theologization of Kabbalah."

10. Scholem, *Kabbalah*, p. 181.

11. Weber, *Ancient Judaism*, p. 314.

12. Heiler, *Prayer*; Toynbee, *An Historian's Approach to Religion*.

13. Zaehner, *At Sundry Times*, p. 171.

14. McGinn, *The Foundations of Mysticism*; Idel, *Kabbalah*.

15. Lewis, *Our Experience of God*; Bastide, *The Mystical Life*.

16. Lorberbaum, *The Image of God*.

17. Pedaya, *Vision and Speech*; Uffenheimer, *The Ancient Prophecy in Israel*; Uffenheimer, *Classical Prophecy*; Kreisel, *Prophecy*; Rahman, *Prophecy in Islam*; Wolfson, *Philo*.

18. Naeh, " 'Creates the Fruit of Lips.' "

19. Idel, *Kabbalah*; Idel, *Hasidism*; Pedaya, *Vision and Speech*; Garb, *Manifestations of Power in Jewish Mysticism*; Idel, *Enchanted Chains*; Mark, *Mysticism and Madness*; Wolfson, *Through a Speculum That Shines*.

20. Idel, *Hasidism*; Idel, *Enchanted Chains*.

21. Couliano, *Experiences de l'extase*; Lewis, *Ecstatic Religion*; Arzy, Idel et al., "Speaking with One's Self"; Blanke and Mohr, "Out-of-Body Experience, Heautoscopy, and Autoscopic Hallucination"; Brugger, "Reflective Mirrors."

22. Blackmore, *Beyond the Body*; Blackmore, *Dying to Live*; Arzy and Blanke, "Out-of-Body, Out-of-Time"; Blanke, Landis et al., Out-of-Body Experience and Autoscopy"; Irwin, *Flight of Mind*; Gallagher, "Philosophical Conceptions of the Self"; Blanke and Metzinger, "Full-Body Illusions and Minimal Phenomenal Selfhood"; Metzinger, *Being No One*; Neisser, "Five Kinds of Self-Knowledge."

23. Frederiks, "Disorders of the Body Schema"; Hécaen and Ajuriaguerra, *L'Heautoscopie, meconnassiances et hallucinations corporelles*; Menninger-Lerchenthal, *Das Truggebilde der Eigenen Gestalt*; Sollier, *Les phenomenes d'autoscopie*; Critchley, *The Parietal Lobes*; Arzy, Overney et al., "Neural Mechanisms of Embodiment"; Feinberg, Haber, and Leeds, "Verbal Asomatognosia"; Feinberg and Roane, "Delusional Misidentification"; Weinstein et al., "Phenomenon of reduplication"; Weinstein, "The Classification of Delusional Misidentification Syndromes"; Peer, Lyon, and Arzy, "Orientation and Disorientation."

24. Ramachandran and Hirstein, "The Perception of Phantom Limbs"; Botvinick and Cohen, "Rubber Hands 'Feel' Touch That Eyes See"; Ehrsson, Holmes, and Passingham, "Touching a Rubber Hand"; Arzy, Seeck et al.,

"Induction of an Illusory Shadow Person"; Blanke, Ortigue, Landis, and Seeck, "Stimulating Illusory Own-Body Perceptions"; Blackmore, *Beyond the Body*.
   25. Gallagher, "Philosophical Conceptions of the Self"; Chaminade and Decety, "Leader or Follower?"; Farrer and Frith, "Experiencing Oneself"; Ruby and Decety, "Effect of Subjective Perspective Taking"; Saxe and Kanwisher, "People Thinking About Thinking People"; Maguire et al., "Knowing Where and Getting There"; Vogeley and Fink, "Neural Correlates of the First-Person-Perspective"; Arzy, Thut et al., "Neural Basis of Embodiment"; Blanke, "Multisensory Brain Mechanisms of Bodily Self-Consciousness."
   26. Eliade, *The Quest*.

3

The One out There

1. Forman, "What Does Mysticism Have to Teach Us?"; Hollenback, *Mysticism*; Idel, *Kabbalah*; Metzinger, *Being No One*; Metzinger, "The Pre-Scientific Concept of a 'Soul.'"
   2. Arzy, Idel et al., "Speaking with One's Self."
   3. Brugger, Regard, and Landis, "Illusory Reduplication"; Dening and Berrios, "Autoscopic Phenomena"; Lukianowicz, "Autoscopic Phenomena"; Blanke, Arzy, and Landis, "Illusory Perceptions"; Blanke and Mohr, "Out-of-Body Experience, Heautoscopy, and Autoscopic Hallucination"; Brugger, "Reflective Mirrors"; Grüsser and Landis, *The Splitting of "I" and "Me"*.
   4. Idel, *Hasidism*; Idel, "Jewish Magic"; Idel, *The Mystical Experience in Abraham Abulafia*; Idel, *Natan Ben Sa'adyah Har'ar (Sha'arei Tzedeq)*; Idel, *Ascensions on High*.
   5. Idel, "On the Theologization of Kabbalah"; Idel, *Kabbalah*; Arzy, Idel et al., "Speaking with One's Self."
   6. Dening and Berrios, "Autoscopic Phenomena"; Blanke, Landis et al., "Out-of-Body Experience and Autoscopy"; Grüsser and Landis, *The Splitting of "I" and "Me"*; Critchley, *The Parietal Lobes*; Frederiks, "Disorders of the Body Schema"; Hécaen and Ajuriaguerra, *L'Heautoscopie, meconnassiances et hallucinations corporelles*; Menninger-Lerchenthal, *Das Truggebilde Der Eigenen Gestalt*.
   7. Irwin, *Flight of Mind*, case 1.
   8. Brugger, Agosti et al., "Heautoscopy, Epilepsy, and Suicide."
   9. Blackmore, *Beyond the Body*.

10. Idel, *The Mystical Experience in Abraham Abulafia*; Dietrich, *Eine Mithrasliturgie*; Meirovitch, *Mystique et poesie en Islam*; Reitzenstein, *Die Hellenistischen Mysterienreligionen*; Scholem, *On the Mystical Shape of the Godhead*; Couliano, *Out of This World*; Gyatso, *Guide to Dakini Land*; Pangborn, *Zoroastrianism*.

11. Idel, "Jewish Magic"; Eco, *Foucault's Pendulum*; Scholem, *The Kabbalah of Sefer Hatemuna*; Wirszubski, "Liber Redemptionis."

12. Zimmer, "On the Significance of the Indian Tantric Yoga"; Idel, *Enchanted Chains*; Gyatso, *Guide to Dakini Land*; Forman, "What Does Mysticism Have to Teach Us?"; Hollenback, *Mysticism*; Idel, *Kabbalah*.

13. Idel, *The Mystical Experience in Abraham Abulafia*; Idel, *Language, Torah, and Hermeneutics*; Pines, "Foreword"; Scholem, "Golem."

14. Bowers and Glasner, "Autohypnotic Aspects."

15. Irwin, *Flight of Mind*, p. 280.

16. Arzy, Thut et al., "Neural Basis of Embodiment"; Blanke, Mohr et al., "Linking Out-of-Body Experience"; Palmer, "ESP and Out-of-Body Experiences"; Pylyshyn, "The Rate of 'Mental Rotation' of Images"; Zacks et al., "Imagined Transformations of Bodies."

17. Abulafia, *Imrei Shefer*, p. 49.

18. Abulafia, *Sefer ha-Hesheq*, fol. 8a.

19. Abulafia, *Sitrei Torah*, fol. 158a.

20. Abulafia, *Otzar Eden Ganuz*, fols. 163b–164a; see also Abulafia, *Hayei Haolam Haba*, fol. 12a.

21. Abulafia, *Otzar Eden Ganuz*, fols. 163b–164a.

22. Har'ar, *Sha'arei Tzedeq*, fols. 64b–65a.

23. Arzy, Idel et al., "Speaking with One's Self"; Idel, *The Mystical Experience in Abraham Abulafia*; Idel, *Natan Ben Sa'adyah Har'ar (Sha'arei Tzedeq)*.

24. Idel, *Ascensions on High*; Couliano, *Out of This World*.

25. Smith, "Ascents to Heavens"; Smith, *Clement of Alexandria and a Secret Gospel of Mark*, p. 56.

26. Arzy, Idel et al., "Why Revelations Have Occurred on Mountains?"

27. Levin, "Otzar ha-Geonim," pp. 14–15.

28. Benayahu, *Sefer Toldot ha-Ari*, p. 155.

29. Vital, *Sha'arei Qedusha*, fol. 16a.

30. Ibid.

31. Idel, *Ascensions on High*; Mondshine, "Sefer Migdal 'Oz"; Idel, *Hasidism*; Eliade, *Shamanism*.

32. Quoted in Caird, *The Evolution of Theology in the Greek Philosophers II*, p. 214.

33. Idel, *The Mystical Experience in Abraham Abulafia*.

34. Anonymous, *Sefer ha-Tzeruf*, fol. 187a.

35. Goldreich, *Sefer Meirat Einayim*, p. 217.

36. Idel, *R. Menahem Recanati; Beur ha-Torah*, fol. 37d.

37. Anonymous, *Ma'arekheth ha-'Elohuth*, fol. 98c.

38. Abulafia, *Sefer ha-Hesheq*, fol. 9a (New York) and fols. 12a–12b (British Library).

39. Abulafia, *Sefer Hayei Haolam Haba*, fol. 56b.

40. Abulafia, *Sefer ha-Oth*, pp. 81–82.

41. Ibid.

42. Steffens and Grube, "Phenomenology of Heautoscopy."

43. Moshe, *Shushan Sodot*, fol. 69b.

44. Ibid.

45. Har'ar, *Sha'arei Tzedeq*, fol. 73a.

46. Ibid., fols. 64b–65a.

47. Ibid., fols. 63b–64a.

48. Dening and Berrios, "Autoscopic Phenomena."

49. Har'ar, *Sha'arei Tzedeq*, fol. 65a.

50. Blanke, Arzy, and Landis, "Illusory Perceptions"; Blanke, Ortigue, Coeytaux et al., "Hearing of a Presence."

51. Brugger, Regard, Landis, and Oelz, "Hallucinatory Experiences."

52. Idel, *The Mystical Experience in Abraham Abulafia*; Scholem, "R. Moshe of Burgos," chap. 27, sec. 4.

53. Shmuel, *Otzar Hayim*, fols. 162b–163a.

54. Idel, *Natan Ben Sa'adyah Har'ar (Sha'arei Tzedeq)*; quotation from Scholem, *On the Mystical Shape of the Godhead*, p. 253—54.

55. Qalqish, *Even Sapir*, fols. 158a–158b.

56. Vajda, *R. Yehuda ben-Nissim ibn-Malka*, pp. 22–23.

57. Brugger, "Reflective Mirrors"; Sollier, *Les phenomenes d'autoscopie*; Zamboni, Budriesi, and Nichelli, " 'Seeing Oneself' "; Féré, "Note sur les hallucinations autoscopiques."

58. Anonymous, *Sefer ha-Hayim*, Oxford-Bodleiana 574, fol. 13b.

59. Ibid., Oxford-Bodleiana 1954, fol. 68a.

60. Ibid., Oxford-Bodleiana 1574, fol. 34b.

61. Quoted in Faierstein, *Jewish Mystical Autobiographies*, p. 116.

62. Quoted in Safrin, *Rabbi Hayim Vital*, pp. 102–3, 114–15.

63. Green, *Out-of-Body Experiences*; Blackmore, *Dying to Live*; Couliano, *Psychanodia I*; Eliade, *Shamanism*; Couliano, *Out of This World*; Irwin, *Flight of Mind*; Blanke and Mohr, "Out-of-Body Experience, Heautoscopy, and Autoscopic Hallucination"; Muldoon and Carrington, *The Projection of the Astral Body*.

64. Safrin, *Zohar Hai* 3, fol. 129d.

65. Mondshine, *Shivehei ha-Besht*, pp. 235–36.

66. Mondshine, *Sefer Migdal 'Oz*, p. 124.

67. Quoted in Porush, *Sullam ha-'Aliyah*, p. 73.

68. Quoted in Dov Baer of Mezeritch, *Magid Devarav le-Ya'akov*, pp. 38–39.

69. Scholem, *On the Mystical Shape of the Godhead*.

70. Devinsky, Feldmann et al., "Autoscopic Phenomena with Seizures," case 4.

71. Dewhurst and Pearson, "Visual Hallucinations of the Self in Organic Disease"; Irwin, *Flight of Mind*; Lukianowicz, "Autoscopic Phenomena."

72. Har'ar, *Sha'arei Tzedeq*, fols. 48b–49a.

73. Muldoon and Carrington, *The Projection of the Astral Body*; Irwin, *Flight of Mind*; Lukianowicz, "Autoscopic Phenomena"; Blanke, Landis et al., "Out-of-Body Experience and Autoscopy."

74. Williams, "The Structure of Emotions Reflected in Epileptic Experiences"; Lunn, "Autoscopic Phenomena"; Brugger, Regard, Landis, and Oelz, "Hallucinatory Experiences"; Blanke, Ortigue, Landis, and Seeck, "Stimulating Illusory Own-Body Perceptions"; Hécaen and Ajuriaguerra, *L'Heautoscopie, meconnassiances et hallucinations corporelles*; Dening and Berrios, "Autoscopic Phenomena"; Devinsky, Feldmann et al., "Autoscopic Phenomena with Seizures"; Lukianowicz, "Autoscopic Phenomena"; Blanke, Arzy, and Landis, "Illusory Perceptions."

75. Arzy, Thut et al., "Neural Basis of Embodiment"; Blanke, Mohr et al., "Linking Out-of-Body Experience"; see also Zacks et al., "Imagined Transformations of Bodies"; Arzy, Mohr et al., "Duration and Not Strength of Activation"; Parsons, "Imagined Spatial Transformation of One's Body"; Ratcliff, "Spatial Thought."

76. Downing et al., "A Cortical Area Selective for Visual Processing"; Astafiev et al., "Extrastriate Body Area"; Saxe, Jamal, and Powell, "My Body or Yours?"; Jeannerod, "Visual and Action Cues"; Peelen and Downing, "Is the Extrastriate Body Area Involved?"; Arzy, Thut et al., "Neural Basis of Embodiment."

77. Arzy, Thut et al., "Neural Basis of Embodiment"; Leube et al., "The Neural Correlates of Perceiving One's Own Movements"; Ruby and Decety, "Effect of Subjective Perspective Taking"; Vogeley and Fink, "Neural Correlates of the First-Person-Perspective"; Saxe and Kanwisher, "People Thinking about Thinking People"; Farrell and Robertson, "The Automatic Updating"; Farrer and Frith, "Experiencing Oneself"; Maguire et al., "Knowing Where and Getting There."

78. Idel, *Natan Ben Saʿadyah Harʾar (Shaʾarei Tzedeq)*, p. 27; translated by Scholem, *Major Trends in Jewish Mysticism*, p. 155, in a different manner.

79. Buckner and Carroll, "Self-projection and the brain"; Arzy et al., "Subjective Mental Time."

80. Grossman and Blake, "Brain Areas Active"; Grill-Spector and Malach, "The Human Visual Cortex"; Urgesi, Berlucchi, and Aglioti, "Magnetic Stimulation"; Arzy, Arzouan et al., "The 'Intrinsic' System"; Decety and Sommerville, "Shared Representations Between Self and Other"; Frith and Dolan, "Brain Mechanisms Associated with Top-Down Processes in Perception."

81. Dening and Berrios, "Autoscopic Phenomena"; Devinsky, Feldmann et al., "Autoscopic Phenomena with Seizures"; Lukianowicz, "Autoscopic Phenomena"; Blanke and Metzinger, "Full-Body Illusions and Minimal Phenomenal Selfhood"; Brugger, Regard, and Landis, "Illusory Reduplication"; Hécaen and Ajuriaguerra, *L'Heautoscopie, meconnassiances et hallucinations corporelles*; Féré, "Note sur les hallucinations autoscopiques"; Blanke, Ortigue, Landis, and Seeck, "Stimulating Illusory Own-Body Perceptions"; Lunn, "Autoscopic Phenomena."

82. Pugh et al., "Cerebral Organization of Component Processes in Reading"; Temple et al., "Disrupted Neural Responses"; Xu et al., "Conjoint and Extended Neural Networks"; Cohen et al., "Visual Word Recognition"; Iragui and Kritchevsky, "Alexia Without Agraphia or Hemianopia"; Shaywitz et al., "Functional Disruption"; Shaywitz, "Dyslexia."

83. Arzy, Thut et al., "Neural Basis of Embodiment."

4

The Spirit in the Brain

1. Spiegel, "Dissociative Disorders"; Gelder et al., *Oxford Textbook of Psychiatry*; American Psychiatric Association, *Diagnostic and Statistical Manual*; Berlyne, "Confabulation"; Chu and Dill, "Dissociative Symptoms"; Freinkel, Koopman, and Spiegel, "Dissociative Symptoms"; Putnam et al., "The Clinical Phenomenology of Multiple Personality Disorder"; Silberman et al., "Dissociative States in Multiple Personality Disorder."

2. Chajes, *Between Worlds*; Goldish, "Vision and Possession"; Idel, *Kabbalah*; Patai, "Exorcism and Xenoglossia"; Werblowsky, *Joseph Karo*; Goldish, *Spirit Possession in Judaism*.

3. Arzy, Mohr et al., "Duration and Not Strength of Activation"; Arzy, Mohr, et al., "Schizotypal Perceptual Aberrations of Time."

4. Bourguignon, *Possession*; Lewis-Fernandez and Kleinman, "Culture, Personality, and Psychopathology"; Spiegel, "Dissociative Disorders."

5. Spiegel, "Dissociative Disorders"; Bourguignon, "Spirit Possession Belief and Social Structure"; Lewis-Fernandez and Kleinman, "Culture, Personality, and Psychopathology"; Adityanjee, Raju, and Khandelwal, "Current Status"; Saxena and Prasad, "DSM-III Subclassification"; Khalifa and Hardie, "Possession and Jinn"; Oesterreich, *Die Bessessenheit*; Bourguignon, *Possession*.

6. Chu and Dill, "Dissociative Symptoms"; Freinkel, Koopman, and Spiegel, "Dissociative Symptoms"; Putnam et al., "The Clinical Phenomenology of Multiple Personality Disorder"; Coons and Milstein, "Psychosexual Disturbances"; Herman, Perry, and van der Kolk, "Childhood Trauma"; Madakasira and O'Brien, "Acute Posttraumatic Stress Disorder"; Noyes Jr. and Kletti, "Depersonalization in Response to Life-Threatening Danger"; Marmar et al., "Peritraumatic Dissociation and Posttraumatic Stress."

7. Janet, *The Major Symptoms of Hysteria*. For the functional anatomy of dissociative amnesia, see Arzy et al. "Psychogenic Amnesia and Self-Identity."

8. Bilu, "Dibbuk and Maggid"; Faierstein, "Maggidim"; James, *The Varieties of Religious Experience*; Patai, "Exorcism and Xenoglossia."

9. Bilu, "Dibbuk and Maggid"; Bilu, "The Moroccan Demon in Israel"; Bilu, "The Taming of the Deviants and Beyond"; Patai, "Exorcism and Xenoglossia"; Goldish, *Spirit Possession in Judaism*; Chajes, *Between Worlds*; Bourguignon, "Spirit Possession Belief and Social Structure"; Carpanzano, "Introduction"; Spiro, *Burmese Supernaturalism*; Ullman and Krasner, *A Psychological Approach to Abnormal Behavior*.

10. Pines, "Le Sefer ha-Tamar."

11. Goldish, "Vision and Possession"; Idel, "Inquiries into the Doctrine of Sefer ha-Meshiv"; Patai, "Exorcism and Xenoglossia"; Bilu, "Dibbuk and Maggid."

12. Werblowsky, *Joseph Karo*, pp. 258–60.

13. Benayahu, *Sefer Toldot ha-Ari*.

14. Werblowsky, *Joseph Karo*, p. 80.

15. Benayahu, *Sefer Toldot ha-Ari*.

16. Fine, "Recitation of Mishnah as a Vehicle"; Fine, *Physician of the Soul*; Bilu, "Dibbuk and Maggid."

17. Sabbatai, *Sefer 'Avodath Yisra'el*, fol. 99a.

18. Quoted in Jacobs, *The Schocken Book of Jewish Mystical Testimonies*, pp. 123–26.

19. Quoted in Kalus, "Lurianic Texts," pp. 408–13.

20. Quoted in Freiman, *Injane Sabbatai Zewi*, p. 45.

21. Scholem, *Sabbatai Sevi*.

22. Quoted in Freiman, *Injane Sabbatai Zewi*, pp. 74–75.

23. Bourguignon, *Possession*.

24. Bilu, "The Taming of the Deviants and Beyond."

25. Chomsky, *Rules and Representations*; Kihlstrom, "The Cognitive Unconscious."

26. Damasio, *The Feeling of What Happens*; Hilgard, *Divided Consciousness*; Li, "A Neural Network Model of Dissociative Disorders"; Janet, *The Major Symptoms of Hysteria*.

27. Janet, *The Major Symptoms of Hysteria*; American Psychiatric Association, *Diagnostic and Statistical Manual*.

28. Schacter, *Searching for Memory*, pp. 151, 17.

29. Solms and Turnbull, *The Brain and the Inner World*.

30. Arzy, Arzouan et al., "The 'Intrinsic' System."

31. Schnider, "Spontaneous Confabulation, Reality Monitoring"; Schnider, "Spontaneous Confabulation and the Adaptation of Thought"; Berlyne, "Confabulation."

32. Huntjens et al., "Procedural Memory in Dissociative Identity Disorder."

33. Picard and Craig, "Ecstatic Epileptic Seizures"; Asheim Hansen and Brodtkorb, "Partial Epilepsy with 'Ecstatic' Seizures"; Cirignotta, Todesco, and Lugaresi, "Temporal Lobe Epilepsy with Ecstatic Seizures."

34. Schacter, *Searching for Memory*; Squire, Stark, and Clark, "The Medial Temporal Lobe"; Corkin, "What's New with the Amnesic Patient H.M.?"

35. Wheeler, Stuss, and Tulving, "Toward a Theory of Episodic Memory."

36. Forrest, "Toward an Etiology of Dissociative Identity Disorder."

37. Ibid.; Frith and Frith, "Interacting Minds"; Gusnard, Akbudak et al., "Medial Prefrontal Cortex"; Reinders et al., "One Brain, Two Selves"; Arzy, Molnar-Szakacs, and Blanke, "Self in Time"; Arzy, Collette et al., "Subjective Mental Time"; Ingvar, " 'Memory of the Future' "; Fuster, *The Prefrontal Cortex*; Starkstein and Robinson, "Mechanism of Disinhibition after Brain Lesions."

38. Burgess et al., "A Temporoparietal and Prefrontal Network"; Levine et al., "The Functional Neuroanatomy of Episodic and Semantic Autobiographical Remembering"; Addis, Wong, and Schacter, "Remembering the Past and Imagining the Future"; Atance and O'Neill, "Episodic Future Thinking"; Schacter, Addis, and Buckner, "Remembering the Past to Imagine the Future"; Tulving, "Episodic Memory"; Buckner and Carroll, "Self-Projection and the Brain"; Ruby and Decety, "Effect of Subjective Perspective Taking"; Vogeley

and Fink, "Neural Correlates of the First-Person-Perspective"; Zacks et al., "Imagined Transformations of Bodies"; Arzy, Thut et al., "Neural Basis of Embodiment"; Farrer and Frith, "Experiencing Oneself."

39. Arzy, Seeck et al., "Induction of an Illusory Shadow Person"; Blanke, Arzy, and Landis, "Illusory Perceptions"; Brugger, Regard, and Landis, "Illusory Reduplication"; Critchley, "The Idea of a Presence."

Conclusions

1. Idel, *Ascensions on High*.

2. Idel, "On mobility, individuals and groups."

3. This approach found its expression in our first joint work, published in the *Journal of Consciousness Studies* in 2005 (Arzy, Idel et al., "Speaking with One's Self"), and is now extensively expressed in this book; Idel, *Enchanted Chains*.

4. Arzy, Arzouan et al., "The 'Intrinsic' System."

Appendix A. The External and Internal Worlds

1. Waxman, *Clinical Neuroanatomy*.

2. Mesulam, *Principles of Behavioral and Cognitive Neurology*; Mesulam, "From Sensation to Cognition."

3. Ibid.; Macaluso and Driver, "Multisensory Spatial Interactions"; Achard et al., "A Resilient, Low-Frequency, Small-World Human Brain Functional Network."

4. Vaadia et al., "Dynamics of Neuronal Interactions"; Behrens and Sporns, "Human Connectomics"; Phillips and Singer, "In Search of Common Foundations for Cortical Computation."

5. Mesulam, "Large-Scale Neurocognitive Networks"; Yeo et al., "The Organization of the Human Cerebral Cortex."

6. Solms and Turnbull, *The Brain and the Inner World*; Critchley, *The Parietal Lobes*; Spiers, Maguire, and Burgess, "Hippocampal Amnesia"; Bird, Vargha-Khadem, and Burgess, "Impaired Memory"; Mesulam, *Principles of Behavioral and Cognitive Neurology*.

7. Bechara et al., "Double Dissociation of Conditioning and Declarative Knowledge"; LeDoux, *The Emotional Brain*.

8. Naghavi and Nyberg, "Common Fronto-Parietal Activity."

9. Ungerleider and Mishkin, "Two Cortical Visual Systems"; Damasio, Damasio, and Van Hoesen, "Prosopagnosia"; Johnson, "Subcortical Face Processing"; Stone and Valentine, "Accuracy of Familiarity Decisions."

10. Mesulam, *Principles of Behavioral and Cognitive Neurology*; Solms and Turnbull, *The Brain and the Inner World*; Penfield and Evans, "The Frontal Lobe in Man"; Damasio, Grabowski et al., "The Return of Phineas Gage"; Rao, Rainer, and Miller, "Integration of What and Where"; Baddeley, *Working Memory*, 1986; Baddeley, "Working Memory," 1992; Desimone, "Neural Mechanisms"; Gusnard, Akbudak et al., "Medial Prefrontal Cortex"; Tulving, "Episodic Memory."

11. Critchley, *The Parietal Lobes*; Maguire et al., "Knowing Where and Getting There"; Arzy, Thut et al., "Neural Basis of Embodiment"; Blanke and Arzy, "The Out-of-Body Experience"; Blanke, Mohr et al., "Linking Out-of-Body Experience"; Downing et al., "A Cortical Area Selective for Visual Processing"; Leube et al., "The Neural Correlates"; Ruby and Decety, "Effect of Subjective Perspective Taking"; Springer and Deutsch, *Left Brain, Right Brain*; Vogeley and Fink, "Neural Correlates of the First-Person-Perspective"; Zacks et al., "Imagined Transformations of Bodies."

12. Heilman, Valenstein, and Watson, "Neglect and Related Disorders"; Robertson and Marshall, *Unilateral Neglect*.

13. Arzy, Overney et al., "Neural Mechanisms of Embodiment"; Feinberg, Haber, and Leeds, "Verbal Asomatognosia"; Nightingale, "Somatoparaphrenia"; Vuilleumier, "Anosognosia"; Solms and Turnbull, *The Brain and the Inner World*.

14. Squire, Stark, and Clark, "The Medial Temporal Lobe"; McGaugh, "The Amygdala Modulates"; LeDeux, *The Emotional Brain*.

15. Mesulam, *Principles of Behavioral and Cognitive Neurology*; Mesulam, "Large-Scale Neurocognitive Networks"; Damasio, "Time-Locked Multiregional Retroactivation."

16. van Hoesen, "The Parahippocampal Gyrus"; McClelland, "The Organization of Memory."

17. Tulving, "Memory and Consciousness"; Tulving, "Episodic Memory"; Wheeler, Stuss, and Tulving, "Toward a Theory of Episodic Memory"; Levine et al., "The Functional Neuroanatomy."

18. Ford and Folks, "Conversion Disorders: An Overview"; Marshall et al., "The Functional Anatomy of a Hysterical Paralysis"; Breuer and Freud, *Studies in Hysteria*; Saj et al., "Disturbance in Mental Imagery."

19. Papez, "A Proposed Mechanism of Emotion"; Granziera et al., "In-Vivo Magnetic Resonance Imaging."

20. Hutsler and Galuske, "Hemispheric Asymmetries."

21. Blanke and Arzy, "The Out-of-Body Experience"; Springer and Deutsch, *Left Brain, Right Brain*; Adolphs et al., "Cortical Systems for the Recognition of Emotion in Facial Expressions"; Benowitz et al., "Hemispheric

Specialization in Nonverbal Communication"; Kolb and Taylor, "Affective Behavior in Patients with Localized Cortical Excisions."

22. Blanke and Arzy, "The Out-of-Body Experience"; Springer and Deutsch, *Left Brain, Right Brain*; Vogeley and Fink, "Neural Correlates of the First-Person-Perspective"; Mesulam, "From Sensation to Cognition"; Mesulam, "Large-Scale Neurocognitive Networks"; Solms and Turnbull, *The Brain and the Inner World*.

23. Churchland, *Neurophilosophy*.

24. Engel, Fries, and Singer, "Dynamic Predictions"; Goldman-Rakic, "Topography of Cognition"; Llinas et al., "The Neuronal Basis for Consciousness."

25. Desimone and Duncan, "Neural Mechanisms of Selective Visual Attention"; Miller and Cohen, "An Integrative Theory of Prefrontal Cortex Function"; Raichle, MacLeod et al., "A Default Mode of Brain Function"; Raichle and Snyder, "A Default Mode of Brain Function"; Schall, "Neural Basis of Deciding, Choosing and Acting."

26. Wilson, "Six Views of Embodied Cognition"; Kosslyn, *Image and Brain*; Kosslyn, Ganis, and Thompson, "Neural Foundations of Imagery"; Beer, "Dynamical Approaches to Cognitive Science"; von Stein et al., "Synchronization Between Temporal and Parietal Cortex"; Weiss and Rappelsberger, "Long-Range EEG Synchronization"; Wilson et al., "Listening to Speech Activates Motor Areas."

27. Rizzolatti and Valese, "Mirror Neurons."

28. Arzy, Arzouan et al., "The 'Intrinsic' System."

29. Varela et al., "The Brainweb."

30. Fox et al., "The Human Brain Is Intrinsically Organized"; Golland, Bentin et al., "Extrinsic and Intrinsic Systems"; Golland, Golland et al., "Data-Driven Clustering"; Arzy, Arzouan et al., "The 'Intrinsic' System."

31. Varela et al., "The Brainweb."

32. Treisman, "Solutions to the Binding Problem."

33. E.g. Stein, Meredith, and Wallace, "The Visually Responsive Neuron and Beyond."

34. Varela et al., "The Brainweb"; Mesulam, "Large-Scale Neurocognitive Networks."

35. Miller, "The Prefrontal Cortex and Cognitive Control"; Frith and Dolan, "Brain Mechanisms Associated with Top-down Processes in Perception."

36. Mesulam, "From Sensation to Cognition"; Mesulam, "Large-Scale Neurocognitive Networks."

37. Baars, "The Conscious Access Hypothesis"; Baars, Ramsoy, and Laureys, "Brain, Conscious Experience and the Observing Self"; Baars and Franklin, "How Conscious Experience and Working Memory Interact."

38. Tononi and Edelman, "Consciousness and Complexity"; Tononi, Sporns, and Edelman, "Reentry and the Problem of Integrating Multiple Cortical Areas"; Sporns et al., "Organization, Development and Function"; Sporns and Kotter, "Motifs in Brain Networks"; Bullmore and Sporns, "Complex Brain Networks."

39. Chafee and Goldman-Rakic, "Inactivation of Parietal and Prefrontal Cortex"; Gray, "The Temporal Correlation Hypothesis"; Riehle et al., "Spike Synchronization and Rate Modulation"; Roelfsema et al., "Visuomotor Integration"; Miltner et al., "Coherence of Gamma-Band EEG Activity."

40. Engel and Singer, "Temporal Binding and the Neural Correlates of Sensory Awareness"; Varela et al., "The Brainweb"; Engel, Fries, and Singer, "Dynamic Predictions"; Fries, "A Mechanism for Cognitive Dynamics."

41. Miltner et al., "Coherence of Gamma-Band EEG Activity"; Engel and Singer, "Temporal Binding and the Neural Correlates of Sensory Awareness"; Rodriguez et al., "Perception's Shadow"; Tallon-Baudry et al., "Oscillatory Gamma-Band (30–70 Hz) Activity"; Keil et al., "Human Gamma Band Activity"; Womelsdorf et al., "Modulation of Neuronal Interactions."

42. Sarnthein et al., "Synchronization Between Prefrontal and Posterior Association Cortex"; von Stein et al., "Synchronization Between Temporal and Parietal Cortex"; Goebel et al., "The Constructive Nature of Vision"; Damasio, "Category-Related Recognition Defects"; Tallon-Baudry et al., "Oscillatory Gamma-Band (30–70 Hz) Activity"; Engel and Singer, "Temporal Binding and the Neural Correlates of Sensory Awareness."

43. Wilson, "Six Views of Embodied Cognition"; Clark, "An Embodied Cognitive Science?"; Coslett, Saffran, and Schwoebel, "Knowledge of the Human Body"; Frith, *Making Up the Mind*.

44. James, *The Principles of Psychology*; Gibson, *The Ecological Approach to Visual Perception*.

45. Chiel and Beer, "The Brain Has a Body"; Thompson and Varela, "Radical Embodiment"; Evans, "Sleep, Consciousness and the Spontaneous and Evoked Electrical Activity of the Brain."

46. Bateson, *Steps to an Ecology of Mind*, p. 242.

47. Damasio, *The Feeling of What Happens*; de Lafuente and Romo, "Neuronal Correlates of Subjective Sensory Experience."

48. Hurely, *Consciousness in Action*; Chiel and Beer, "The Brain Has a Body"; Clark, "An Embodied Cognitive Science?"

49. Gusnard, Akbudak et al., "Medial Prefrontal Cortex"; Raichle and Mintun, "Brain Work and Brain Imaging"; Gusnard and Raichle, "Searching for a Baseline"; Buckner and Carroll, "Self-Projection and the Brain"; Ingvar,

" 'Memory of the Future' "; Raichle, MacLeod et al., "A Default Mode of Brain Function"; Raichle and Snyder, "A Default Mode of Brain Function"; Arzy, Arzouan et al., "The 'Intrinsic' System"; Baars, "The Conscious Access Hypothesis"; Golland, Bentin et al., "Extrinsic and Intrinsic Systems."

    50. Laureys et al., "Impaired Effective Cortical Connectivity in Vegetative State"; Steriade, Timofeev, and Grenier, "Natural Waking and Sleep States"; John et al., "Invariant Reversible QEEG Effects of Anesthetics"; Blumenfeld and Taylor, "Why Do Seizures Cause Loss of Consciousness?"; Massimini et al., "Breakdown of Cortical Effective Connectivity During Sleep"; Baars, Ramsoy, and Laureys, "Brain, Conscious Experience and the Observing Self"; Baars, "The Conscious Access Hypothesis."

    51. Bressler and Kelso, "Cortical Coordination Dynamics and Cognition."

Bibliography

Primary Sources

Abulafia, A. *Imrei Shefer*. Ms. Paris, Bibliothèque nationale de France 777.
———. *Hayei Haolam Haba*. Ms. Oxford-Bodleiana 1582.
———. *Otzar Eden Ganuz*. Ms. Oxford-Bodleiana 1580.
———. *Sefer ha-Hesheq*. Ms. New York, Jewish Theological Seminary, 1801, fol. 9a; Ms. London, British Library 749, fols. 12a–12b.
———. *Sefer ha-Oth*, Jerusalem, 2001. In English: *Sefer Ha-Ot: The Book of the Sign*. Providence University, 2007.
———. *Sefer Hayei Haolam Haba*. Ms. Oxford-Bodleiana 1582.
———. *Sitrei Torah*. Ms. Paris, Bibliothèque nationale de France 774.
Anonymous. *Ma'arekheth ha-'Elohuth*. Mantua, 1558.
Anonymous. *Sefer ha-Hayim*. Ms. Oxford-Bodleiana 574, 1954, 1574.
Anonymous. *Sefer ha-Tzeruf*. Ms. Munich 22.
Dov Baer of Mezeritch. 1976. *Maggid Devarav le-Ya'akov*. Ed. R. Schatz-Uffenheimer. Jerusalem: Magnes.
Goldreich, A., ed. 1981. *Sefer Meirat Einayim*. Jerusalem: Hebrew University.
Har'ar, Nathan ben Sa'adyah. *Sha'arei Tzedeq*. Ms. Jerusalem, Jewish National and University Library, 148 8°.
Levin, B., ed. 1932. *Otzar ha-Geonim*. Jerusalem.
Moshe of Kiev. *Shushan Sodot*. Ms. Oxford-Bodleiana 1655.
Recanati, Menahem. *Beur ha-Torah*.
Qalqish, Elnathan ben-Moshe. *Even Sapir*. Ms. Paris, Bibliothèque nationale de France 727.

Sabbatai, Israel ben. *Sefer 'Avodath Yisra'el*. Munkacz 1928.

Safrin, Isaac, of Komarno. *Zohar Hai* 3. Available at http://www.hebrewbooks. org/20311.

Shmuel, Isaac ben. *Otzar Hayim*, Ms. Moscow-Ginsburg 775.

Vajda, Y. A., ed. 1974. *R. Yehuda ben-Nissim ibn-Malka, Kitab Uns Utafsir*. Ramat Gan: Bar-Ilan University.

Vital, Hayim. *Sha'arei Qedusha*. Ms. British Library 749.

Secondary Sources

Achard, S., R. Salvador, B. Whitcher, J. Suckling, and E. Bullmore. 2006. "A resilient, low-frequency, small-world human brain functional network with highly connected association cortical hubs." *J Neurosci* 26 (1):63–72.

Addis, D. R., A. T. Wong, and D. L. Schacter. 2007. "Remembering the past and imagining the future: common and distinct neural substrates during event construction and elaboration." *Neuropsychologia* 45 (7):1363–77.

Adityanjee, G. S. Raju, and S. K. Khandelwal. 1989. "Current status of multiple personality disorder in India." *Am J Psychiatry* 146 (12):1607–10.

Adolphs, R., H. Damasio, D. Tranel, and A. R. Damasio. 1996. "Cortical systems for the recognition of emotion in facial expressions." *J Neurosci* 16 (23):7678–87.

American Psychiatric Association. 2000. *Diagnostic and Statistical Manual of Mental Disorders*. 4th ed. Washington, DC: American Psychiatric Press.

Arzy, S., Y. Arzouan, E. Adi-Japha, S. Solomon, and O. Blanke. 2010. The "intrinsic" system in the human cortex and self-projection: a data driven analysis. *Neuroreport* 21, 569–74.

Arzy, S., and O. Blanke. 2005. "Out-of-body, out-of-time: abnormal unity of body and self in space and time." In *Endophysics, Time, Quantum, and the Subjective*, edited by R. Buccheri, A. Elitzur, and M. Sanniga, 507–30. Hackensack, NJ: World Scientific.

Arzy, S., S. Collette, S. Ionta, E. Fornari, O. Blanke. 2009. "Subjective mental time: the functional architecture of projecting the self to past and future." *Eur J Neurosci* 30(10):2009–17.

Arzy, S., S. Collette, M. Wissmeyer, F. Lazeyras, P. W. Kaplan, O. Blanke. 2011. "Psychogenic amnesia and self-identity: a multimodal functional investigation." *Eur J Neurol* 18:1422–25.

Arzy, S., M. Idel, T. Landis, and O. Blanke. 2005. "Speaking with one's self: autoscopic phenomena in the ecstatic Kabbalah of the 13th century." *Journal of Consciousness Studies* 12:4–29.

————. 2005. "Why revelations have occurred on mountains? Linking mystical experiences and cognitive neuroscience." *Med Hypotheses* 65 (5):841–45.

Arzy, S., C. Mohr, C. M. Michel, and O. Blanke. 2007. "Duration and not strength of activation in temporo-parietal cortex positively correlates with schizotypy." *Neuroimage* 35 (1):326–33.

Arzy, S., C. Mohr, I. Molnar-Szakacs, and O. Blanke. 2011. "Schizotypal perceptual aberrations of time: correlation between score, behavior and brain activity." *PLoS One* 6 (1):e16154.

Arzy, S., I. Molnar-Szakacs, and O. Blanke. 2008. "Self in time: imagined self-location influences neural activity related to mental time travel." *J Neurosci* 28 (25):6502–7.

Arzy, S., L. S. Overney, T. Landis, and O. Blanke. 2006. "Neural mechanisms of embodiment: asomatognosia due to premotor cortex damage." *Arch Neurol* 63 (7):1022–25.

Arzy, S., M. Seeck, S. Ortigue, L. Spinelli, and O. Blanke. 2006. "Induction of an illusory shadow person." *Nature* 443 (7109):287.

Arzy, S., G. Thut, C. Mohr, C. M. Michel, and O. Blanke. 2006. "Neural basis of embodiment: distinct contributions of temporoparietal junction and extrastriate body area." *J Neurosci* 26 (31):8074–81.

Asheim Hansen, B., and E. Brodtkorb. 2003. "Partial epilepsy with 'ecstatic' seizures." *Epilepsy Behav* 4:667–73.

Astafiev, S. V., C. M. Stanley, G. L. Shulman, and M. Corbetta. 2004. "Extrastriate body area in human occipital cortex responds to the performance of motor actions." *Nat Neurosci* 7 (5):542–48.

Atance, C. M., and D. K. O'Neill. 2001. "Episodic future thinking." *Trends Cogn Sci* 1, 5 (12):533–39.

Baars, B. J. 2002. "The conscious access hypothesis: origins and recent evidence." *Trends Cogn Sci* 6 (1):47–52.

Baars, B. J., and S. Franklin. 2003. "How conscious experience and working memory interact." *Trends Cogn Sci* 7 (4):166–72.

Baars, B. J., T. Z. Ramsoy, and S. Laureys. 2003. "Brain, conscious experience and the observing self." *Trends Neurosci* 26 (12):671–75.

Baddeley, A. 1986. *Working Memory*. Oxford: Oxford University Press.

————. 1992. "Working memory." *Science* 255 (5044):556–59.

Bastide, R. 1935. *The Mystical Life*. Translated by D. Waring and H. F. Kynaston-Snell. New York: Scribner.

Bateson, G. 1999. *Steps to an Ecology of Mind*. Chicago: University of Chicago Press.

Bechara, A., D. Tranel, H. Damasio, R. Adolphs, C. Rockland, and A. R. Damasio. 1995. "Double dissociation of conditioning and declarative knowledge relative to the amygdala and hippocampus in humans." *Science* 269 (5227):1115–18.

Beer, R. D. 2000. "Dynamical approaches to cognitive science." Trends Cogn Sci 4 (3):91–99.

Behrens, T. E., and O. Sporns. 2012. "Human connectomics." *Curr Opin Neurobiol* 22 (1):144–53.

Ben Shlomo, J. 1994. "Gershom Scholem on pantheism in the Kabbalah." In *Gershom Scholem: The Man and His Work*, edited by P. Mendes-Flohr, 60–61. Albany, NY: University of New York Press.

Benayahu, M. 1960. *Sefer Toldot ha-Ari*. Jerusalem: Machon ben-Zvi.

Benowitz, L. I., D. M. Bear, R. Rosenthal, M. M. Mesulam, E. Zaidel, and R. W. Sperry. 1983. "Hemispheric specialization in nonverbal communication." *Cortex* 19 (1):5–11.

Berlucchi, G., and S. Aglioti. 1997. "The body in the brain: neural bases of corporeal awareness." *Trends Neurosci* 20 (12):560–64.

Berlyne, N. 1972. "Confabulation." *Br J Psychiatry* 120 (554):31–39.

Bilu, Y. 1980. "The Moroccan Demon in Israel: the case of "evil spirit disease." *Ethos* 8:24–39.

———. 1985. "The taming of the deviants and beyond: an analysis of Dybbuqk possession and exorcism in Judaism." *Psychoanalytic Study of Society* 11:1–32.

———. 1996. "Dibbuk and Maggid: two cultural patterned of altered consciousness in Judaism." *AJS Review* 21:341–66.

Bird, C. M., F. Vargha-Khadem, and N. Burgess. 2008. "Impaired memory for scenes but not faces in developmental hippocampal amnesia: a case study." *Neuropsychologia* 46 (4):1050–59.

Blackmore, S. J. 1982. *Beyond the Body: An Investigation of Out-of-Body Experiences*. London: Heinemann.

———. 1993. *Dying to Live: Science and the Near-Death Experience*. London: Grafton

Blanke, O. 2004. "Illusions visuelles." In *Neuro-Ophtalmologie*, edited by A. B. Safran, A. Vighetto, T. Landis, and E. Cabanis, 147–50. Paris: Masson.

———. 2012. "Multisensory brain mechanisms of bodily self-consciousness." *Nat Rev Neurosci* 13 (8):556–71.

Blanke, O., and S. Arzy. 2005. "The out-of-body experience: disturbed self-processing at the temporo-parietal junction." *Neuroscientist* 11 (1):16–24.

Blanke, O., S. Arzy, and T. Landis. 2008. "Illusory perceptions of the human body and self." In *Handbook of Clinical Neurology: Neuropsychology and Behavioral Neurology*, edited by G. Goldenberg and B. Miller, 429–58. Amsterdam: Elsevier.

Blanke, O., T. Landis, L. Spinelli, and M. Seeck. 2004. "Out-of-body experience and autoscopy of neurological origin." *Brain* 127 (pt 2):243–58.

Blanke, O., and T. Metzinger. 2009. "Full-body illusions and minimal phenomenal selfhood." *Trends Cogn Sci* 13 (1):7–13.

Blanke, O., and C. Mohr. 2005. "Out-of-body experience, heautoscopy, and autoscopic hallucination of neurological origin: implications for neurocognitive mechanisms of corporeal awareness and self-consciousness." *Brain Res Brain Res Rev* 50 (1):184–99.

Blanke, O., C. Mohr, C. M. Michel, A. Pascual-Leone, P. Brugger, M. Seeck, T. Landis, and G. Thut. 2005. "Linking out-of-body experience and self processing to mental own-body imagery at the temporoparietal junction." *J Neurosci* 25 (3):550–57.

Blanke, O., S. Ortigue, A. Coeytaux, M. D. Martory, and T. Landis. 2003. "Hearing of a presence." *Neurocase* 9 (4):329–39.

Blanke, O., S. Ortigue, T. Landis, and M. Seeck. 2002. "Stimulating illusory own-body perceptions." *Nature* 419 (6904):269–70.

Blumenfeld, H., and J. Taylor. 2003. "Why do seizures cause loss of consciousness?" *Neuroscientist* 9 (5):301–10.

Botvinick, M., and J. Cohen. 1998. "Rubber hands 'feel' touch that eyes see." *Nature* 391 (6669):756.

Bourguignon, E. 1976. *Possession*. Corta Madera, CA: Chandler and Sharp.

———. 1976. "Spirit possession belief and social structure." In *The Realm of the Extra-Human: Ideas and Actions*, edited by A. Bahrti, 17–26. Paris: Mouton.

Bowers, M., and S. Glasner. 1958. "Autohypnotic aspects of the Kabbalistic concept of Kavana." *Journal of Clinical and Experimental Hypnosis* 6:3–23.

Bressler, S. L., and J. A. Kelso. 2001. "Cortical coordination dynamics and cognition." *Trends Cogn Sci* 5 (1):26–36.

Breuer, J., and S. Freud. 2004. *Studies in Hysteria*. Penguin Modern Classics. London: Penguin. First published 1895.

Brugger, P. 2002. "Reflective mirrors: perspective-taking in autoscopic phenomena." *Cognitive Neuropsychiatry* 7 (3):179–94.

Brugger, P., R. Agosti, M. Regard, H. G. Wieser, and T. Landis. 1994. "Heautoscopy, epilepsy, and suicide." *J Neurol Neurosurg Psychiatry* 57 (7):838–39.

Brugger, P., M. Regard, and T. Landis. 1997. "Illusory reduplication of one's own body: phenomenology and classification of autoscopic phenomena." *Cognitive Neuropsychiatry* 2:19–38.

Brugger, P., M. Regard, T. Landis, and O. Oelz. 1999. "Hallucinatory experiences in extreme-altitude climbers." *Neuropsychiatry Neuropsychol Behav Neurol* 12 (1):67–71.

Buber, M. 1996. *Ecstatic Confessions: The Heart of Mysticism.* Translated by E. Cameron. Edited by Paul Mendes-Flohr. Syracuse, NY: First Syracuse University Press.

Buckner, R. L., and D. C. Carroll. 2007. "Self-projection and the brain." *Trends Cogn Sci* 11 (2):49–57.

Bullmore, E., and O. Sporns. 2009. "Complex brain networks: graph theoretical analysis of structural and functional systems." *Nat Rev Neurosci* 10 (3):186–98.

Burgess, N., E. A. Maguire, H. J. Spiers, J. O'Keefe. 2001. "A temporoparietal and prefrontal network for retrieving the spatial context of lifelike events." *Neuroimage* 14 (2):439–53.

Burkert, W. 1983. *Homo Necans: The Anthropology of Ancient Greek Sacrificial Ritual and Myth.* Translated by P. Bing. Berkeley: University of California Press.

Caird, A. 1904. *The Evolution of Theology in the Greek Philosophers II.* Glasgow: Lames MacLehose and Sons (reprint 2006, Kessinger Publishing).

Carpanzano, V. 1977. "Introduction." In *Case Studies in Spirit Possession*, edited by V. Carpanzano and V. Gattison, 1–40. New York: John Wiley and Sons.

Chafee, M. V., and P. S. Goldman-Rakic. 2000. "Inactivation of parietal and prefrontal cortex reveals interdependence of neural activity during memory-guided saccades." *J Neurophysiol* 83 (3):1550–66.

Chajes, J. H. 2003. *Between Worlds: Dybbuks, Exorcists, and Early Modern Judaism.* Philadelphia: University of Pennsylvania Press.

Chaminade, T., and J. Decety. 2002. "Leader or follower?: involvement of the inferior parietal lobule in agency." *Neuroreport* 13 (15):1975–78.

Chiel, H. J., and R. D. Beer. 1997. "The brain has a body: adaptive behavior emerges from interactions of nervous system, body and environment." *Trends Neurosci* 20 (12):553–57.

Chomsky, N. 1980. *Rules and Representations.* New York: Columbia University Press.

Chu, J. A., and D. L. Dill. 1990. "Dissociative symptoms in relation to childhood physical and sexual abuse." *Am J Psychiatry* 147 (7):887–92.

Churchland, P. 1986. *Neurophilosophy.* Cambridge, MA: MIT Press.

Cirignotta F., C. V. Todesco, E. Lugaresi. 1980. "Temporal lobe epilepsy with ecstatic seizures (so-called Dostoevsky epilepsy)." *Epilepsia* 21:705–10.

Clark, A. 1999. "An embodied cognitive science?" *Trends Cogn Sci* 3 (9):345–51.

Cohen, L., and S. Dehaene. 2004. "Specialization within the ventral stream: the case for the visual word form area." *Neuroimage* 22 (1):466–76.

Cohen, L., O. Martinaud, C. Lemer, S. Lehericy, Y. Samson, M. Obadia, A. Slachevsky, and S. Dehaene. 2003. "Visual word recognition in the left and right hemispheres: anatomical and functional correlates of peripheral alexias." *Cereb Cortex* 13 (12):1313–33.

Coons, P. M., and V. Milstein. 1986. "Psychosexual disturbances in multiple personality: characteristics, etiology, and treatment." *J Clin Psychiatry* 47 (3):106–10.

Corkin, S. 2002. "What's new with the amnesic patient H.M.?" *Nat Rev Neurosci* 3 (2):153–60.

Coslett, H. B., E. M. Saffran, and J. Schwoebel. 2002. "Knowledge of the human body: a distinct semantic domain." *Neurology* 59 (3):357–63.

Couliano, I. P. 1983. *Psychanodia I: A Survey of the Evidence Concerning the Ascension of the Soul and Its Relevance.* Leiden: Brill.

———. 1984. *Experiences de l'extase.* Paris: Payot.

———. 1991. *Out of This World: Otherworldly Journeys from Gilgamesh to Albert Einstein.* Boston: Shambhala.

Critchley, M. 1953. *The Parietal Lobes.* London: Edward Arnold.

———. 1955. "The idea of a presence." *Acta Psychiatr Neurol Scand* 30 (1–2):155–68.

Critchley, M. 1979. *The Divine Banquet of the Brain and Other Essays.* New York: Raven.

Damasio, A. 1999. *The Feeling of What Happens.* London: Heinemann.

Damasio, A. R. 1989. "Time-locked multiregional retroactivation: a systems-level proposal for the neural substrates of recall and recognition." *Cognition* 33 (1–2):25–62.

———. 1990. "Category-related recognition defects as a clue to the neural substrates of knowledge." *Trends Neurosci* 13 (3):95–98.

Damasio, A. R., H. Damasio, and G. W. Van Hoesen. 1982. "Prosopagnosia: anatomic basis and behavioral mechanisms." *Neurology* 32 (4):331–41.

Damasio, H., T. Grabowski, R. Frank, A. M. Galaburda, and A. R. Damasio. 1994. "The return of Phineas Gage: clues about the brain from the skull of a famous patient." *Science* 264 (5162):1102–5.

de Lafuente, V., and R. Romo. 2005. "Neuronal correlates of subjective sensory experience." *Nat Neurosci* 8 (12):1698–1703.

de Souzenelle, A. 1991. *Le symbolisme du corps humain*. Paris: Michel Albin.

Decety, J., and J. A. Sommerville. 2003. "Shared representations between self and other: a social cognitive neuroscience view." *Trends Cogn Sci 7* (12):527–33.

Deikman, A. J. 1962. "Deautomatization and the mystic experience." In *Altered States of Consciousness*, edited by C. T. Tart, 25–46. New York: Doubleday.

Dening, T. R., and G. E. Berrios. 1994. "Autoscopic phenomena." *Br J Psychiatry* 165 (6):808–17.

Desimone, R. 1996. "Neural mechanisms for visual memory and their role in attention." *Proc Natl Acad Sci USA* 93 (24):13494–99.

Desimone, R., and J. Duncan. 1995. "Neural mechanisms of selective visual attention." *Annu Rev Neurosci* 18:193–222.

Devinsky, O., E. Feldmann, K. Burrowes, and E. Bromfield. 1989. "Autoscopic phenomena with seizures." *Arch Neurol* 46 (10):1080–88.

Devinsky, O., F. Putnam, J. Grafman, E. Bromfield, and W. H. Theodore. 1989. "Dissociative states and epilepsy." *Neurology* 39 (6):835–40.

Dewhurst, K., and J. Pearson. 1955. "Visual hallucinations of the self in organic disease." *J Neurol Neurosurg Psychiatry* 18 (1):53–57.

Dietrich, A. 1923. *Eine Mithrasliturgie*. Leipzig: B. G. Teubner.

Downing, P. E., Y. Jiang, M. Shuman, and N. Kanwisher. 2001. "A cortical area selective for visual processing of the human body." *Science* 293 (5539):2470–73.

Durkheim, E. 1965. *The Elementary Forms of the Religious Life*. Translated by J. Swain. New York: The Free Press.

Eco, U. 1989. *Foucault's Pendulum*. New York: Harcourt.

Ehrsson, H. H., N. P. Holmes, and R. E. Passingham. 2005. "Touching a rubber hand: feeling of body ownership is associated with activity in multisensory brain areas." *J Neurosci* 25 (45):10564–73.

Ehrsson, H. H., C. Spence, and R. E. Passingham. 2004. "That's my hand!: activity in premotor cortex reflects feeling of ownership of a limb." *Science* 305 (5685):875–77.

Eliade, M. 1958. *Rites and Symbols of Initiation*. Translated by W.R. Trask. New York: Harper.

Eliade, M. 1960. *Myths, Dreams, and Mysteries*. Translated by P. Mairet. New York: Harper Torchbooks.

———. 1969. *The Two and the One*. London: Harvell.

———. 1969. *Yoga, Immortality and Freedom*. Princeton, NJ: Princeton University Press.

———. 1971. *The Quest: History and Meaning in Religion:* Chicago: University of Chicago Press.

————. 1972. *Zalmoxis*. Translated by W. R. Trask. Chicago: University of Chicago Press.

————. 1974. *Shamanism: Archaic Techniques of Ecstasy*. Princeton, NJ: Princeton University Press.

Engel, A. K., P. Fries, and W. Singer. 2001. "Dynamic predictions: oscillations and synchrony in top-down processing." *Nat Rev Neurosci* 2 (10):704–16.

Engel, A. K., and W. Singer. 2001. "Temporal binding and the neural correlates of sensory awareness." *Trends Cogn Sci* 5 (1):16–25.

Etkes, I. 2000. *Ba'al Hashem, the Besht: Magic, Mysticism, Leadership*. Jerusalem: Zalman Shazar Center for Jewish History

Evans, B. M. 2003. "Sleep, consciousness and the spontaneous and evoked electrical activity of the brain. Is there a cortical integrating mechanism?" *Neurophysiol Clin* 33 (1):1–10.

Faierstein, M. M. 1999. *Jewish Mystical Autobiographies*. New York: Paulist Press.

————. 2003. "Maggidim, spirits and women in Rabbi Hayyim Vital's *Book of Visions*." In *Spirit Possession in Judaism*, edited by M. Goldish, 186–96. Detroit: Wayne State University Press.

Farrell, M. J., and I. H. Robertson. 2000. "The automatic updating of egocentric spatial relationships and its impairment due to right posterior cortical lesions." *Neuropsychologia* 38 (5):585–95.

Farrer, C., N. Franck, N. Georgieff, C. D. Frith, J. Decety, and M. Jeannerod. 2003. "Modulating the experience of agency: a positron emission tomography study." *Neuroimage* 18 (2):324–33.

Farrer, C., and C. D. Frith. 2002. "Experiencing oneself vs another person as being the cause of an action: the neural correlates of the experience of agency." *Neuroimage* 15 (3):596–603.

Feinberg, T. E., L. D. Haber, and N. E. Leeds. 1990. "Verbal asomatognosia." *Neurology* 40 (9):1391–94.

Feinberg, T. E., and D. M. Roane. 2005. "Delusional misidentification." *Psychiatr Clin North Am* 28 (3):665–83.

Féré, C. 1891. "Note sur les hallucinations autoscopiques ou speculaires et sur les hallucinations altruistes." *C. R. Seance Sociale Biologie* 3:451–53.

Fine, L. 1982. "Recitation of Mishnah as a vehicle for mystical inspiration: a contemplative technique taught by Hayyim Vital." *Revue des Études Juives* (141):193.

————. 2003. *Physician of the Soul, Healer of the Cosmos: Isaac Luria and His Kabbalistic Fellowship*. Palo Alto, CA: Stanford University Press.

Ford, C. V., and D. G. Folks. 1985. "Conversion disorders: an overview." *Psychosomatics* 26 (5):371–74, 380–83.

Forman, R. K. C. 1998. "What does mysticism have to teach us about consciousness?" *Journal of Consciousness Studies* 5:185–201.

Forrest, K. A. 2001. "Toward an etiology of dissociative identity disorder: a neurodevelopmental approach." *Conscious Cogn* 10 (3):259–93.

Fox, M. D., A. Z. Snyder, J. L. Vincent, M. Corbetta, D. C. Van Essen, and M. E. Raichle. 2005. "The human brain is intrinsically organized into dynamic, anticorrelated functional networks." *Proc Natl Acad Sci USA* 102 (27):9673–78.

Frederiks, J. A. M. 1969. "Disorders of the body schema." In *Handbook of Neurology*, edited by P. J. Vinken and G. W. Bruyn, 207–40. Amsterdam: North-Holland.

Freiman, A. 1912. *Injane Sabbatai Zewi*. Berlin: Mekize Nirdamim.

Freinkel, A., C. Koopman, and D. Spiegel. 1994. "Dissociative symptoms in media eyewitnesses of an execution." *Am J Psychiatry* 151 (9):1335–39.

Fries, P. 2005. "A mechanism for cognitive dynamics: neuronal communication through neuronal coherence." *Trends Cogn Sci* 9 (10):474–80.

Frith, C. 1996. "The role of the prefrontal cortex in self-consciousness: the case of auditory hallucinations." *Philos Trans R Soc Lond B Biol Sci* 351 (1346):1505–12.

———. 2007. *Making Up the Mind: How the Brain Creates Our Mental World*. Oxford: Wiley-Blackwell.

Frith, C., and R. J. Dolan. 1997. "Brain mechanisms associated with top-down processes in perception." *Philos Trans R Soc Lond B Biol Sci* 352 (1358):1221–30.

Frith, C. D., and U. Frith. 1999. "Interacting minds—a biological basis." *Science* 286 (5445):1692–95.

Fu, K. M., T. A. Johnston, A. S. Shah, L. Arnold, J. Smiley, T. A. Hackett, P. E. Garraghty, and C. E. Schroeder. 2003. "Auditory cortical neurons respond to somatosensory stimulation." *J Neurosci* 23 (20):7510–15.

Fuster, J. M. 1997. *The Prefrontal Cortex: Anatomy, Physiology, and Neuropsychology of the Frontal Lobe*. 3rd ed. Philadelphia: Lippincott-Raven.

Gallagher, S. 2000. "Philosophical conceptions of the self: implications for cognitive science." *Trends Cogn Sci* 4:14–21.

Garb, J. 2004. *Manifestations of Power in Jewish Mysticism*. Jerusalem: Magnes.

Garb, J. 2011. *Shamanic Trance in Modern Kabbalah*. Chicago: University of Chicago Press.

Gelder, M., D. Gath, R. Mayou, and P. Cowen. 2001. *Oxford Textbook of Psychiatry*. 3rd ed. New York: Oxford University Press.

Gibson, J. J. 1979. *The Ecological Approach to Visual Perception*. Boston: Houghton-Mifflin.

Goebel, R., D. Khorram-Sefat, L. Muckli, H. Hacker, and W. Singer. 1998. "The constructive nature of vision: direct evidence from functional magnetic resonance imaging studies of apparent motion and motion imagery." *Eur J Neurosci* 10 (5):1563–73.

Goldish, M. 2003. "Vision and possession: Nathan of Gaza's earliest prophecies in historical context." In *Spirit Possession in Judaism*, edited by M. Goldish, 217–236. Detroit: Wayne State University Press.

———, ed. 2003. *Spirit Possession in Judaism: Cases and Contexts from the Middle Ages to the Present*. Detroit: Wayne State University Press.

Goldman-Rakic, P. S. 1988. "Topography of cognition: parallel distributed networks in primate association cortex." *Annu Rev Neurosci* 11:137–56.

Golland, Y., S. Bentin, H. Gelbard, Y. Benjamini, R. Heller, Y. Nir, U. Hasson, and R. Malach. 2007. "Extrinsic and intrinsic systems in the posterior cortex of the human brain revealed during natural sensory stimulation." *Cereb Cortex* 17 (4):766–77.

Golland, Y., P. Golland, S. Bentin, and R. Malach. 2008. "Data-driven clustering reveals a fundamental subdivision of the human cortex into two global systems." *Neuropsychologia* 46 (2):540–53.

Granziera, C., N. Hadjikhani, S. Arzy, M. Seeck, G. Meuli, G. Krueger. 2011. "In-Vivo Magnetic Resonance Imaging of the Structural Core of the Papez Circuit in Humans." *Neuroreport*. 22 (5):227–31.

Grave de Peralta Menendez, R., S. Gonzalez Andino, G. Lantz, C. M. Michel, and T. Landis. 2001. "Noninvasive localization of electromagnetic epileptic activity. I. Method descriptions and simulations." *Brain Topogr* 14 (2):131–37.

Grave de Peralta Menendez, R., M. M. Murray, C. M. Michel, R. Martuzzi, and S. L. Gonzalez Andino. 2004. "Electrical neuroimaging based on biophysical constraints." *Neuroimage* 21 (2):527–39.

Gray, C. M. 1999. "The temporal correlation hypothesis of visual feature integration: still alive and well." *Neuron* 24 (1):31–47, 111–25.

Green, C. E. 1968. *Out-of-Body Experiences*. Oxford: Institute of Psychophysical Research.

Grill-Spector, K., and R. Malach. 2004. "The human visual cortex." *Annu Rev Neurosci* 27:649–77.

Grossman, E. D., and R. Blake. 2002. "Brain areas active during visual perception of biological motion." *Neuron* 35 (6):1167–75.

Gruenwald, I. 1989. "From Talmudic to Zoharic homiletics." In *The Age of the Zohar*, edited by J. Dan, 255–98. Jerusalem: Jerusalem National and University Library.

Grüsser, O. J., and T. Landis. 1991. *The Splitting of "I" and "Me": Heautoscopy and Related Phenomena, Visual Agnosias and Other Disturbances of Visual Perception and Cognition.* Amsterdam: Macmillan.

Gusnard, D. A., E. Akbudak, G. L. Shulman, and M. E. Raichle. 2001. "Medial prefrontal cortex and self-referential mental activity: relation to a default mode of brain function." *Proc Natl Acad Sci USA* 98 (7):4259–64.

Gusnard, D. A., and M. E. Raichle. 2001. "Searching for a baseline: functional imaging and the resting human brain." *Nat Rev Neurosci* 2 (10):685–94.

Gyatso, G. K. 1996. *Guide to Dakini Land: The Highest Yoga Tantra Practice of Buddha Vajrayogini.* London: Tharpa.

Hadot, P. 1993. "Exercices spirituels et philosophie antique." *Annuaire de la Vᵉ section de l'école pratique des hautes études, Paris* 84:25–70.

———. 1995. *Qu'est-ce que la philosophie antique?* Paris: Folio.

Halligan, P. W., G. R. Fink, J. C. Marshall, and G. Vallar. 2003. "Spatial cognition: evidence from visual neglect." *Trends Cogn Sci* 7 (3):125–33.

Halligan, P. W., and J. C. Marshall. 1998. "Neglect of awareness." *Conscious Cogn* 7 (3):356–80.

Hausherr, I. 1929. "La methode d'Oraison Hesychaste." *Orientalia Christiana* 9:128–29.

Hécaen, H., and J. Ajuriaguerra. 1952. *L'Heautoscopie, meconnassiances et hallucinations corporelles.* Paris: Masson.

Heiler, F. 1933. *Prayer: A Study of the History and Psychology of Religion.* London.

Heilman, K. M., E. Valenstein, and R. T. Watson. 2000. "Neglect and related disorders." *Semin Neurol* 20 (4):463–70.

Hellner-Eshed, M. 2005. *"A River Issues Forth from Eden": On the Language of Mystical Experience in the Zohar.* Tel Aviv: Am-Oved.

Herman, J. L., J. C. Perry, and B. A. van der Kolk. 1989. "Childhood trauma in borderline personality disorder." *Am J Psychiatry* 146 (4):490–95.

Heschel, A. J. 1962. *The Prophets.* New York: Harper and Row.

Hilgard, E. R. 1977. *Divided Consciousness: Multiple Controls in Human Thought and Action.* New York: Wiley and Sons.

Hollenback, J. B. 1996. *Mysticism: Experience, Response, and Empowerment.* University Park: Pennsylvania State University Press.

Huntjens, R. J., A. Postma, L. Woertman, O. van der Hart, and M. L. Peters. 2005. "Procedural memory in dissociative identity disorder: when can inter-identity amnesia be truly established?" *Conscious Cogn* 14 (2):377–89.

Hurely, S. 1998. *Consciousness in Action*. Cambridge, MA: Harvard University Press.

Hutsler, J., and R. A. Galuske. 2003. "Hemispheric asymmetries in cerebral cortical networks." *Trends Neurosci* 26 (8):429–35.

Idel, M. 1983. "Inquiries into the doctrine of Sefer ha-Meshiv." *Sefunot* 17:185–266.

———. 1988. *The Mystical Experience in Abraham Abulafia*. Translated by J. Chipman. Albany: State University of New York Press.

———. 1989. "Jewish magic from the Renaissance period to early Hasidism." In *Religion, Science, and Magic: In Concert and in Conflict*, edited by J. Neusner, E. S. Frerichs, and P. V. M. Flesher, 107–8. New York: Oxford University Press.

———. 1989. *Language, Torah, and Hermeneutics in Abraham Abulafia*. Translated by M. Kallus. Albany: State University of New York Press.

———. 1990. *Kabbalah: New Perspectives*. New Haven, CT: Yale University Press.

———. 1991. "Between Rabbinism and Kabbalism: Gershom Scholem's phenomenology of Judaism." *Modern Judaism* 11:281–96.

———. 1992. " 'Unio mystica' as a criterion: 'Hegelian' phenomenologies of Jewish mysticism." In *Doors of Understanding: Conversations in Global Spirituality*, edited by S. Chase, 303–33. Quincy, IL.: Franciscan Press.

———. 1993. "Defining Kabbalah: The Kabbalah of the divine names." In *Mystics of the Book: Themes, Topics, and Typologies*, edited by R. A. Herrera, 97–99. New York: Peter Lang.

———. 1993. "Some remarks on ritual, mysticism, and Kabbalah in Gerone." *Journal for Jewish Thought and Philosophy* 3:111–13.

———. 1995. *Hasidism: Between Ecstasy and Magic*. Albany: State University of New York Press.

———. 1998. "On mobility, individuals and groups: prolegomenon for a sociological approach to sixteenth-century Kabbalah." *Kabbalah* 3:145–73.

———. 1998. *R. Menahem Recanati, the Kabbalist*. Jerusalem: Schocken.

———. 2001. *Natan ben Sa'adyah Har'ar, le Porte della Giustizia (Sha'arei Tzedeq)*. Translated by M. Mottolese. Milano: Adelphi.

———. 2002. "On the meanings of the term 'Kabbalah': between the prophetic Kabbalah and the Kabbalah of Sefirot in the 13th Century." *Pe'amim* 93:69–73.

———. 2003. "On some forms of order in Kabbalah." *Daat* 50–52:31–58.

———. 2004. "Nishmat 'Eloha: on the divinity of the soul in Nahmanides and his school." In *Life as a Midrash: Perspectives in Jewish Psychology*, edited by S. Arzy, M. Fachler, and B. Kahana, 338–80. Tel Aviv: Yediot Ahronot.

———. 2004. "On prophecy and early Hasidism." In *Studies in Modern Religions, Religious Movements, and Babi-Baha'i Faiths*, edited by M. Sharon, 41–75. Leiden: Brill.

———. 2004. "On the theologization of Kabbalah in modern scholarship." In *Religious Apologetics—Philosophical Argumentation*, edited by Y. Schwartz and V. Krech, 123–74. Tübingen: Mohr.

———. 2005. *Ascensions on High in Jewish Mysticism*. Budapest: Central European University Press.

———. 2005. *Enchanted Chains: Techniques and Rituals in Jewish Mysticism*. Los Angeles: Cherub.

———. 2008. "On the language of ecstatic experiences in Jewish mysticism." In *Religionen—Die Religiöse Erfahrung [Religions—The Religious Experience]*, edited by M. Riedl and T. Schabert. Eranos Jahrbuch 74. Würzburg: Königshausen and Neumann, 2008.

———. 2008. "Adonai Sefatai Tiftah: Models of understanding prayer in early Hasidism." *Kabbalah* 18: 7–11.

———. 2008. "On the language of ecstatic experiences in Jewish mysticism." In *Religionen—Die Religiöse Erfahrung*, edited by M. Riedl and T. Schabert, 43–84. Würzburg: Verlag Königshausen & Neumann.

Ingvar, D. H. 1985. " 'Memory of the future': an essay on the temporal organization of conscious awareness." *Hum Neurobiol* 4 (3):127 36.

Iragui, V. J., and M. Kritchevsky. 1991. "Alexia without agraphia or hemianopia in parietal infarction." *J Neurol Neurosurg Psychiatry* 54 (9):841–42.

Irwin, H. J. 1985. *Flight of Mind: A Psychological Study of the Out-of-Body Experience*. Metuchen, NJ: Scarecrow.

Jacobs, L. 1978. *Hasidic Prayer*. New York: Schocken.

———. 1996. *The Schocken Book of Jewish Mystical Testimonies*. New York: Schocken.

James, W. 1890. *The Principles of Psychology*. Cambridge, MA: Harvard University Press.

———. 1961. *The Varieties of Religious Experience*. New York: Collier Macmillan.

Janet, P. 1920. *The Major Symptoms of Hysteria*. New York: Macmillan.

Jeannerod, M. 2004. "Visual and action cues contribute to the self-other distinction." *Nat Neurosci* 7 (5):422–23.

John, E. R., L. S. Prichep, W. Kox, P. Valdes-Sosa, J. Bosch-Bayard, E. Aubert, M. Tom, F. di Michele, and L. D. Gugino. 2001. "Invariant reversible QEEG effects of anesthetics." *Conscious Cogn* 10 (2):165–83.

Johnson, M. H. 2005. "Subcortical face processing." *Nat Rev Neurosci* 6 (10):766–74.

Kalus, M. 2003. "Lurianic texts concerning Rabbi Hayyim Vital and his psychical experience." In *Spirit Possession in Judaism*, edited by M. Goldish, 408–13. Detroit: Wayne State University Press.

Kanwisher, N., J. McDermott, and M. M. Chun. 1997. "The fusiform face area: a module in human extrastriate cortex specialized for face perception." *J Neurosci* 17:4302–11.

Keil, A., M. M. Müller, W. J. Ray, T. Gruber, and T. Elbert. 1999. "Human gamma band activity and perception of a gestalt." *J Neurosci* 15:7152–61.

Kellehear, A. 1990. "The near-death experience as status passage." *Soc Sci Med* 31 (8):933–99.

Khalifa, N., and T. Hardie. 2005. "Possession and jinn." *J R Soc Med* 98 (8):351–53.

Khazaal, Y., G. Zimmermann, and D. F. Zullino. 2005. "Depersonalization—current data." [In French]. *Can J Psychiatry* 50 (2):101–7.

Kihlstrom, J. F. 1987. "The cognitive unconscious." *Science* 237 (4821):1445–52.

Kolb, B., and L. Taylor. 1981. "Affective behavior in patients with localized cortical excisions: role of lesion site and side." *Science* 214 (4516):89–91.

Kosslyn, S. M. 1994. *Image and Brain: The Resolution of the Imagery Debate.* Cambridge, MA: MIT Press.

Kosslyn, S. M., G. Ganis, and W. L. Thompson. 2001. "Neural foundations of imagery." *Nat Rev Neurosci* 2 (9):635–42.

Kreisel, H. 2001. *Prophecy: The History of an Idea in Medieval Jewish Philosophy.* Dordrecht: Kluwer.

Laski, M. 1961. *Ecstasy in Secular and Religious Experiences.* Los Angeles: Tarcher.

Laureys, S., S. Goldman, C. Phillips, P. Van Bogaert, J. Aerts, A. Luxen, G. Franck, and P. Maquet. 1999. "Impaired effective cortical connectivity in vegetative state: preliminary investigation using PET." *Neuroimage* 9 (4):377–82.

Lawson, E. T., and R. N. McCauley. 1993. *Rethinking Religion: Connecting Cognition and Culture.* New York: Cambridge University Press.

LeDeux, J. 1996. *The Emotional Brain.* New York: Simon and Schuster.

Lenggenhager, B., T. Tadi, T. Metzinger, and O. Blanke. 2007. "Video ergo sum: manipulating bodily self-consciousness." *Science* 317 (5841):1096–99.

Leube, D. T., G. Knoblich, M. Erb, W. Grodd, M. Bartels, and T. T. Kircher. 2003. "The neural correlates of perceiving one's own movements." *Neuroimage* 20 (4):2084–90.

Levine, B., G. R. Turner, D. Tisserand, S. J. Hevenor, S. J. Graham, and A. R. McIntosh. 2004. "The functional neuroanatomy of episodic and semantic autobiographical remembering: a prospective functional MRI study." *J Cogn Neurosci* 16 (9):1633–46.

Lewis, H. D. 1959. *Our Experience of God*. London: George Allen and Unwin.

Lewis, I. M. 1971. *Ecstatic Religion: An Anthropological Study of Spirit Possession and Shamanism*. Hammondsworth: Penguin.

Lewis-Fernandez, R., and A. Kleinman. 1994. "Culture, personality, and psychopathology." *J Abnorm Psychol* 103 (1):67–71.

Li, D., and D. Spiegel. 1992. "A neural network model of dissociative disorders." *Psychiatric Annals* 22 (3):144–47.

Liebes, Y. 1992. "Kivunim Hadashim be-Heker ha-Kabbalah." *Pe'amim* 50:150–70.

Llinas, R., U. Ribary, D. Contreras, and C. Pedroarena. 1998. "The neuronal basis for consciousness." *Philos Trans R Soc Lond B Biol Sci* 353 (1377):1841–49.

Lorberbaum, Y. 2004. *The Image of God: Halakhah and Aggadah*. Tel Aviv: Schocken.

Lukianowicz, N. 1958. "Autoscopic phenomena." *AMA Arch Neurol Psychiatry* 80 (2):199–220.

Lunn, V. 1970. "Autoscopic phenomena." *Acta Psychiatria Scandinavia* 46:118–25.

Macaluso, E., and J. Driver. 2005. "Multisensory spatial interactions: a window onto functional integration in the human brain." *Trends Neurosci* 28 (5):264–71.

Madakasira, S., and K. F. O'Brien. 1987. "Acute posttraumatic stress disorder in victims of a natural disaster." *J Nerv Ment Dis* 175 (5):286–90.

Magid, S. "Gershom Scholem's ambivalence toward mystical experience and his critique of Martin Buber in light of Hans Jonas and Martin Heidegger." *Journal of Jewish Thought and Philosophy* 4:245–69.

Maguire, E. A., N. Burgess, J. G. Donnett, R. S. Frackowiak, C. D. Frith, and J. O'Keefe. 1998. "Knowing where and getting there: a human navigation network." *Science* 280 (5365):921–24.

Mark, Z. 2003. *Mysticism and Madness in the Work of R. Nahman of Bratslav*. Tel Aviv: Am Oved and Hartman Institute.

Marmar, C. R., D. S. Weiss, W. E. Schlenger, J. A. Fairbank, B. K. Jordan, R. A. Kulka, and R. L. Hough. 1994. "Peritraumatic dissociation and posttraumatic stress in male Vietnam theater veterans." *Am J Psychiatry* 151 (6):902–7.

Marshall, J. C., P. W. Halligan, G. R. Fink, D. T. Wade, and R. S. Frackowiak. 1997. "The functional anatomy of a hysterical paralysis." *Cognition* 64 (1):B1–8.

Massimini, M., F. Ferrarelli, R. Huber, S. K. Esser, H. Singh, and G. Tononi. 2005. "Breakdown of cortical effective connectivity during sleep." *Science* 309 (5744):2228–32.

Mazoyer, B., L. Zago, E. Mellet, S. Bricogne, O. Etard, O. Houde, F. Crivello, M. Joliot, L. Petit, and N. Tzourio-Mazoyer. 2001. "Cortical networks for working memory and executive functions sustain the conscious resting state in man." *Brain Res Bull* 54 (3):287–98.

McClelland, J. L. 1994. "The organization of memory: a parallel distributed processing perspective." *Rev Neurol (Paris)* 150 (8–9):570–79.

McGaugh, J. L. 2004. "The amygdala modulates the consolidation of memories of emotionally arousing experiences." *Annu Rev Neurosci* 27:1–28.

McGinn, B. 1991. *The Foundations of Mysticism*. New York: Crossroad.

McNamara, Patrick. 2009. *The Neuroscience of Religious Experience*. Cambridge: Cambridge University Press.

Meirovitch, E. 1972. *Mystique et poesie en Islam*. Paris: Desclee de Brouwer.

Menninger-Lerchenthal, E. 1935. *Das Truggebilde der Eigenen Gestalt*. Berlin: Karger.

Merlan, P. 1963. *Monopsychism, Mysticism, Metaconsciousness*. The Hague: Martinus Nijhoff.

Mesulam, M. M. 1990. "Large-scale neurocognitive networks and distributed processing for attention, language, and memory." *Ann Neurol* 28 (5):597–613.

———. 1998. "From sensation to cognition." *Brain* 121 (pt 6):1013–52.

———, ed. 2001. *Principles of Behavioral and Cognitive Neurology*. 2nd ed. Oxford: Oxford University Press.

Metzinger, T. 2003. *Being No One: The Self-Model Theory of Subjectivity*. Cambridge: Bradford.

———. 2005. "The pre-scientific concept of a 'soul': a neurophenomenological hypothesis about its origin." In *Auf der Suche nach dem Konzept/ Substrat der Seele*, edited by M. Peschl, 1–36. Wurzburg: Konigshausen and Neumann.

Michel, C. M., M. M. Murray, G. Lantz, S. Gonzalez, L. Spinelli, and R. Grave de Peralta. 2004. "EEG source imaging." *Clin Neurophysiol* 115 (10):2195–222.

Michel, C. M., G. Thut, S. Morand, A. Khateb, A. J. Pegna, R. Grave de
Peralta, S. Gonzalez, M. Seeck, and T. Landis. 2001. "Electric source
imaging of human brain functions." *Brain Res Brain Res Rev* 36
(2–3):108–18.

Miller, E. K. 2000. "The prefrontal cortex and cognitive control." *Nat Rev
Neurosci* 1 (1):59–65.

Miller, E. K., and J. D. Cohen. 2001. "An integrative theory of prefrontal cortex function." *Annu Rev Neurosci* 24:167–202.

Miller, L. J. 2013. *The Oxford Handbook of Psychology and Spirituality*. Oxford:
Oxford University Press.

Miltner, W. H., C. Braun, M. Arnold, H. Witte, and E. Taub. 1999. "Coherence
of gamma-band EEG activity as a basis for associative learning." *Nature*
397 (6718):434–36.

Mondshine, J., ed. 1980. *Sefer Migdal 'Oz*. Kefar Habad: Makhon Lubawitch.

———, ed. 1982. *Shivehei ha-Besht*. Jerusalem: Hanachal.

Moore, P. 1978. "Mystical experience, mystical doctrine, mystical technique."
In *Mysticism and Philosophical Analysis*, edited by S. T. Katz, 112–14.
New York: Oxford University Press.

Morgan, M. L. 1990. *Platonic Piety: Philosophy and Ritual in Fourth-Century
Athens*. New Haven, CT: Yale University Press.

Muldoon, S. J., and H. Carrington. 1929. *The Projection of the Astral Body*.
London: Rider.

Naeh, S. 1994. " 'Creates the fruit of lips': a phenomenological study of prayer
according to Mishnah Berachot 4:3, 5:5." *Tarbiz* 63:185–218.

Naghavi, H. R., and L. Nyberg. 2005. "Common fronto-parietal activity in
attention, memory, and consciousness: shared demands on integration?" *Conscious Cogn* 14 (2):390–425.

Neisser, U. 1988. "Five kinds of self-knowledge." *Philosophical Psychology* 1.1:
35–59.

Newberg, A. B. 2010. *Principles of Neuroethology*. Surrey: Ashgate.

Nightingale, S. 1982. "Somatoparaphrenia: a case report." *Cortex* 18 (3):463–67.

Noyes, R., Jr., and R. Kletti. 1977. "Depersonalization in response to life-
threatening danger." *Compr Psychiatry* 18 (4):375–84.

Oesterreich, T. K. 1922. *Die Bessessenheit*. Langensalzach: Wendt und
Klauswell.

Palmer, J. 1978. "ESP and out-of-body experiences: an experimental approach."
In *Mind Beyond the Body*, edited by D. S. Rogo, 193–217. Harmond-
sworth: Penguin.

Pangborn, C. R. 1983. *Zoroastrianism: A Beleaguered Faith*. New York: Advent
Books.

Papez, J. W. 1995. "A proposed mechanism of emotion. 1937." *J Neuropsychiatry Clin Neurosci* 7 (1):103–12.

Parsons, L. M. 1987. "Imagined spatial transformation of one's body." *J Exp Psychol Gen* 116 (2):172–91.

Patai, R. 1978. "Exorcism and xenoglossia among the Safed Kabbalists." *Journal of American Folklore* 91:823–35.

Pedaya, H. 2000. "The Besht, R. Jacob Joseph of Polonoy, and the Maggid of Mezeritch: basic lines for a religious-typological approach." *Daat* 45:25–73.

———. 2002. *Vision and Speech: Models of Revelatory Experience in Jewish Mysticism*. Los Angeles: Cherub.

Peelen, M. V., and P. E. Downing. 2005. "Is the extrastriate body area involved in motor actions?" *Nat Neurosci* 8 (2):125; author reply 125–26.

Peer M., R. Lyon, and S. Arzy. 2014. Orientation and disorientation: lessons from patients with epilepsy. *Epilepsy Behav* 41:149–57.

Peer, M., M. Nitzan, I. Goldberg, J. Kats, J. M. Gomori, T. Ben-Hur, and S. Arzy. 2014. "Reversible functional connectivity disturbances during transient global amnesia." *Ann Neurol* 75 (5):634–43.

Penfield, W., and L. Evans. 1935. "The frontal lobe in man: a clinical study of maximal removals." *Brain* 58:115–33.

Penfield, W., and P. Perot. 1963. "The brain's record of auditory and visual experience: a final summary and discussion." *Brain* 86:595–696.

Phillips, W. A., and W. Singer. 1997. "In search of common foundations for cortical computation." *Behav Brain Sci* 20 (4):657–83; discussion 683–722.

Picard, F. and A. D. Craig AD. 2009. "Ecstatic epileptic seizures: a potential window on the neural basis for human self-awareness." *Epilepsy Behav* 16:539–46.

Pike, N. 1992. *Mystic Union: An Essay in the Phenomenology of Mysticism*. Ithaca, NY: Cornell University Press.

Pines, S. 1980. "Le Sefer ha-Tamar et les Maggidim des Kabbalists." In *Hommage à Georges Vajda: Études d'Histoire et de Pensée Juives*, edited by G. Nahon and C. Touati, 333–63. Louvain: Peeters.

———. 1988. "Foreword." In M. Idel, *The Mystical Experience in Abraham Abulafia*, vii–ix. Albany: State University of New York Press.

Podoll, K., and U. Nicola. 2004. "The illness of Giorgio de Chirico—migraine or epilepsy?" *Eur Neurol* 51 (3):186; author reply 186–87.

Porush, Y. E. E, ed. 1989. *Sullam ha-'Aliyah*. Jerusalem: Sha'arei Ziv.

Pugh, K. R., B. A. Shaywitz, S. E. Shaywitz, R. T. Constable, P. Skudlarski, R. K. Fulbright, R. A. Bronen, D. P. Shankweiler, L. Katz, J. M. Fletcher, and J. C. Gore. 1996. "Cerebral organization of component processes in reading." *Brain* 119 (pt 4):1221–38.

Putnam, F. W. 1997. *Dissociation in Children and Adolescents: A Developmental Perspective.* New York: Guilford.

Putnam, F. W., J. J. Guroff, E. K. Silberman, L. Barban, and R. M. Post. 1986. "The clinical phenomenology of multiple personality disorder: review of 100 recent cases." *J Clin Psychiatry* 47 (6):285–93.

Pylyshyn, Z. W. 1979. "The rate of 'mental rotation' of images: a test of a holistic analogue hypothesis." *Mem Cognit* 7 (1):19–28.

Rahman, F. 1958. *Prophecy in Islam.* London: George Allen and Unwin.

Raichle, M. E., A. M. MacLeod, A. Z. Snyder, W. J. Powers, D. A. Gusnard, and G. L. Shulman. 2001. "A default mode of brain function." *Proc Natl Acad Sci USA* 98 (2):676–82.

Raichle, M. E., and M. A. Mintun. 2006. "Brain work and brain imaging." *Annu Rev Neurosci* 29:449–76.

Raichle, M. E., and A. Z. Snyder. 2007. "A default mode of brain function: a brief history of an evolving idea." *Neuroimage* 37 (4):1083–90; discussion 1097–99.

Ramachandran, V. S., and W. Hirstein. 1998. "The perception of phantom limbs: the D. O. Hebb lecture." *Brain* 121 (pt 9):1603–30.

Rank, O. 1925. *Der Doppelganger. Eine Psychoanalytische Studie.* Leipzig: Internationaler Psychoanalytischer Verlag.

Rao, S. C., G. Rainer, and E. K. Miller. 1997. "Integration of what and where in the primate prefrontal cortex." *Science* 276 (5313):821–24.

Ratcliff, G. 1979. "Spatial thought, mental rotation and the right cerebral hemisphere." *Neuropsychologia* 17 (1):49–54.

Reinders, A. A., E. R. Nijenhuis, A. M. Paans, J. Korf, A. T. Willemsen, and J. A. den Boer. 2003. "One brain, two selves." *Neuroimage* 20 (4):2119–25.

Reitzenstein, R. 1927. *Die Hellenistischen Mysterienreligionen.* 3rd ed. Leipzig: J. C. Hinrichs.

Riehle, A., S. Grun, M. Diesmann, and A. Aertsen. 1997. "Spike synchronization and rate modulation differentially involved in motor cortical function." *Science* 278 (5345):1950–53.

Rizzolatti, G., and V. Valese. 2005. "Mirror neurons." *Phenomenology of the Cognitive Sciences* 4:23–48.

Robertson, I. H., and J. C. Marshall, eds. 1993. *Unilateral Neglect: Clinical and Experimental Studies.* London: Lawrence Erlbaum.

Rodriguez, E., N. George, J. P. Lachaux, J. Martinerie, B. Renault, and F. J. Varela. 1999. "Perception's shadow: long-distance synchronization of human brain activity." *Nature* 397 (6718):430–33.

Roelfsema, P. R., A. K. Engel, P. Konig, and W. Singer. 1997. "Visuomotor integration is associated with zero time-lag synchronization among cortical areas." *Nature* 385 (6612):157–61.

Rosman, M. 1996. *Founder of Hasidism: A Quest for the Historical Ba'al Shem Tov*. Berkeley: University of California Press.

Ruby, P., and J. Decety. 2001. "Effect of subjective perspective taking during simulation of action: a PET investigation of agency." *Nat Neurosci* 4 (5):546–50.

Safrin, N., ed. 1988. *Rabbi Hayim Vital—Ketavim Hadashim*. Jerusalem: Ahavat Shalom.

Saj, A., N. Raz, N. Levin, T. Ben-Hur, and S. Arzy. 2014. "Disturbance in mental imagery of affected body-parts in patients with conversion paraplegia demonstrated by functional brain imaging." *Brain Sci* 4 (2):396–404.

Sarnthein, J., H. Petsche, P. Rappelsberger, G. L. Shaw, and A. von Stein. 1998. "Synchronization between prefrontal and posterior association cortex during human working memory." *Proc Natl Acad Sci USA* 95 (12):7092–96.

Saxe, R., N. Jamal, and L. Powell. 2005. "My body or yours?: the effect of visual perspective on cortical body representations." *Cereb Cortex* 16 (2):178–82.

Saxe, R., and N. Kanwisher. 2003. "People thinking about thinking people: the role of the temporo-parietal junction in 'theory of mind.'" *Neuroimage* 19 (4):1835–42.

Saxena, S., and K. V. Prasad. 1989. "DSM-III subclassification of dissociative disorders applied to psychiatric outpatients in India." *Am J Psychiatry* 146 (2):261–62.

Schacter, D. 1996. *Searching for Memory: The Brain, the Mind, and the Past*. New York: Basic Books.

Schacter, D. L., D. R. Addis, and R. L. Buckner. 2007. "Remembering the past to imagine the future: the prospective brain." *Nat Rev Neurosci* 8:657–61.

Schall, J. D. 2001. "Neural basis of deciding, choosing and acting." *Nat Rev Neurosci* 2 (1):33–42.

Schnider, A. 2001. "Spontaneous confabulation, reality monitoring, and the limbic system: a review." *Brain Res Brain Res Rev* 36 (2–3):150–60.

———. 2003. "Spontaneous confabulation and the adaptation of thought to ongoing reality." *Nat Rev Neurosci* 4 (8):662–71.

Scholem, G. 1934. "R. Moshe of Burgos, a student of R. Yitzhak." *Tarbiz* 5.

———. 1971. "Golem." In *Encyclopedia Judaica*, 7:753–56. New York: Macmillan.

———. 1974. *Kabbalah*. Jerusalem: Keter.

———. 1976. *Sabbatai Sevi: The Mystical Messiah*. Translated by R. J. Z. Werblowsky. Princeton, NJ: Princeton University Press.

———. 1991. *On the Mystical Shape of the Godhead*. New York: Schocken.

———. 1991. *Origins of the Kabbalah*. Translated by A. Arkush. Princeton, NJ: Princeton University Press.

———. 1995. *Major Trends in Jewish Mysticism*. New York: Schocken.

Scholem, G. 1969. *The Kabbalah of Sefer Hatemuna and Abraham Abulafia*. Edited by J. Ben-Shlomo. Jerusalem: Academon.

Schroeder, C. E., R. W. Lindsley, C. Specht, A. Marcovici, J. F. Smiley, and D. C. Javitt. 2001. "Somatosensory input to auditory association cortex in the macaque monkey." *J Neurophysiol* 85 (3):1322–27.

Shaywitz, S. E. 1998. "Dyslexia." *N Engl J Med* 338 (5):307–12.

Shaywitz, S. E., B. A. Shaywitz, K. R. Pugh, R. K. Fulbright, R. T. Constable, W. E. Mencl, D. P. Shankweiler, A. M. Liberman, P. Skudlarski, J. M. Fletcher, L. Katz, K. E. Marchione, C. Lacadie, C. Gatenby, and J. C. Gore. 1998. "Functional disruption in the organization of the brain for reading in dyslexia." *Proc Natl Acad Sci USA* 95 (5):2636–41.

Sheils, D. 1978. "A cross-cultural study of beliefs in out-of-the-body experiences, waking and sleeping." *Journal of Sociological & Psychological Research* 49:697–741.

Shoham, G. 2003. *The Mytho-Empiricism of Gnosticism: Triumph of the Vanquished*. Brighton: Sussex Academic Press.

Silberman, E. K., F. W. Putnam, H. Weingartner, B. G. Braun, and R. M. Post. 1985. "Dissociative states in multiple personality disorder: a quantitative study." *Psychiatry Res* 15 (4):253–60.

Smith, J. E. 1968. *Experience and God*. London: Oxford University Press.

Smith, M. 1973. *Clement of Alexandria and a Secret Gospel of Mark*. Cambridge, MA: Harvard University Press.

———. 1981. "Ascents to heavens and the beginning of Christianity." *Eranos Jahrbuch* 50:403–29.

Sollier, P. A. 1903. *Les phenomenes d'autoscopie*. Paris: Felix Alcan.

Solms, M., and O. Turnbull. 2002. *The Brain and the Inner World*. New York: Other Press.

Spiegel, D. 1997. "Dissociative disorders." In *Psychiatry*, edited by A. Tasman, J. Kay, and J. Lieberman. New York: Wiley and Sons.

Spiers, H. J., E. A. Maguire, and N. Burgess. "Hippocampal amnesia." *Neurocase* 7 (5):357–82.

Spiro, M. E. 1967. *Burmese Supernaturalism*. Englewood Cliffs, NJ: Prentice-Hall.

Sporns, O., D. R. Chialvo, M. Kaiser, and C. C. Hilgetag. 2004. "Organization, development and function of complex brain networks." *Trends Cogn Sci* 8 (9):418–25.

Sporns, O., and R. Kotter. 2004. "Motifs in brain networks." *PLoS Biol* 2 (11):e369.

Springer, S. P., and G. Deutsch. 1981. *Left Brain, Right Brain.* San Francisco: Freeman.

Squire, L. R., C. E. Stark, and R. E. Clark. 2004. "The medial temporal lobe." *Annu Rev Neurosci* 27:279–306.

Starkstein, S. E., and R. G. Robinson. 1997. "Mechanism of disinhibition after brain lesions." *J Nerv Ment Dis* 185 (2):108–14.

Steffens, M., and M. Grube. 2001. "Phenomenology of heautoscopy: case report of atypical mirror hallucination." [In German]. *Psychiatr Prax* 28 (4):189–92.

Stein, B. E., M. A. Meredith, and M. T. Wallace. 1993. "The visually responsive neuron and beyond: multisensory integration in cat and monkey." *Prog Brain Res* 95:79–90.

Steriade, M., I. Timofeev, and F. Grenier. 2001. "Natural waking and sleep states: a view from inside neocortical neurons." *J Neurophysiol* 85 (5):1969–85.

Stone, A., and T. Valentine. 2005. "Accuracy of familiarity decisions to famous faces perceived without awareness depends on attitude to the target person and on response latency." *Conscious Cogn* 14 (2):351–76.

Sullivan, L. E. 1988. *Icanchu's Drum: An Orientation to Meaning in South American Religions.* New York: Macmillan.

Tallon-Baudry, C., O. Bertrand, C. Delpuech, and J. Permier. 1997. "Oscillatory gamma-band (30–70 Hz) activity induced by a visual search task in humans." *J Neurosci* 17 (2):722–34.

Temple, E., R. A. Poldrack, J. Salidis, G. K. Deutsch, P. Tallal, M. M. Merzenich, and J. D. Gabrieli. 2001. "Disrupted neural responses to phonological and orthographic processing in dyslexic children: an fMRI study." *Neuroreport* 12 (2):299–307.

Thompson, E., and F. J. Varela. 2001. "Radical embodiment: neural dynamics and consciousness." *Trends Cogn Sci* 5 (10):418–25.

Tononi, G., and G. M. Edelman. 1998. "Consciousness and complexity." *Science* 282 (5395):1846–51.

Tononi, G., O. Sporns, and G. M. Edelman. 1992. "Reentry and the problem of integrating multiple cortical areas: simulation of dynamic integration in the visual system." *Cereb Cortex* 2 (4):310–35.

Toynbee, A. 1956. *An Historian's Approach to Religion*. London: Oxford University Press.

Treisman, A. 1999. "Solutions to the binding problem: progress through controversy and convergence." *Neuron* 24 (1):105–10, 111–25.

Tulving, E. 1985. "Memory and consciousness." *Can Psychol*. 26:1–12.

———. 2002. "Episodic memory: from mind to brain." *Annu Rev Psychol* 53:1–25.

Uffenheimer, B. 1973 *The Ancient Prophecy in Israel*. Jerusalem: Magnes.

———. 2001. *Classical Prophecy: The Prophetic Consciousness*. Jerusalem: Magnes.

Ullman, L. P., and L. Krasner. 1969. *A Psychological Approach to Abnormal Behavior*. Englewood Cliffs, NJ: Prentice-Hall.

Ungerleider, L. G., and M. Mishkin. 1982. "Two cortical visual systems." In *Analysis of Visual Behavior*, edited by D. J. Ingle, M. A. Goodale, and R. J. W. Mansfield, 549–86. Cambridge, MA: MIT Press.

Urgesi, C., G. Berlucchi, and S. M. Aglioti. 2004. "Magnetic stimulation of extrastriate body area impairs visual processing of nonfacial body parts." *Curr Biol* 14 (23):2130–34.

Vaadia, E., I. Haalman, M. Abeles, H. Bergman, Y. Prut, H. Slovin, and A. Aertsen. 1995. "Dynamics of neuronal interactions in monkey cortex in relation to behavioural events." *Nature* 373 (6514):515–18.

van Hoesen, G. W. 1982. "The parahippocampal gyrus: new observations regarding its cortical connections in the monkey." *Trends Neurosci* 5:345–50.

———. 1993. "The modern concept of association cortex." *Curr Opin Neurobiol* 3 (2):150–54.

Varela, F., J. P. Lachaux, E. Rodriguez, and J. Martinerie. 2001. "The brainweb: phase synchronization and large-scale integration." *Nat Rev Neurosci* 2 (4):229–39.

Vogeley, K., and G. R. Fink. 2003. "Neural correlates of the first-person-perspective." *Trends Cogn Sci* 7 (1):38–42.

von Stein, A., P. Rappelsberger, J. Sarnthein, and H. Petsche. 1999. "Synchronization between temporal and parietal cortex during multimodal object processing in man." *Cereb Cortex* 9 (2):137–50.

von Stein, A., and J. Sarnthein. 2000. "Different frequencies for different scales of cortical integration: from local gamma to long range alpha/theta synchronization." *Int J Psychophysiol* 38 (3):301–13.

Vuilleumier, P. 2004. "Anosognosia: the neurology of beliefs and uncertainties." *Cortex* 40 (1):9–17.

Wallis, R. T. 1976. "Nous as experience." In *The Significance of Neoplatonism*, edited by R. Baine Harris, 122–43. Norkfold: International Society for Neoplatonic Studies.

Waxman, S. G. 2003. *Clinical Neuroanatomy*. New York: McGraw-Hill.

Weber, M. 1952. *Ancient Judaism*. Translated by H. H. Gerth and D. Martindale. Glencoe, IL: Free Press.

Weinstein, E., and D. L. Burnham. 1991. "Reduplication and the syndrome of Capgras." *Psychiatry* 54 (1):78–88.

Weinstein, E. A. 1994. "The classification of delusional misidentification syndromes." *Psychopathology* 27 (3–5):130–35.

Weinstein, E. A., R. L. Kahn, and L. A. Sugarman. 1952. "Phenomenon of reduplication." *Arch Neur Psych* 67 (6):808–14.

Weiss, S., and P. Rappelsberger. 2000. "Long-range EEG synchronization during word encoding correlates with successful memory performance." *Brain Res Cogn Brain Res* 9 (3):299–312.

Werblowsky, R. J. Z. 1977. *Joseph Karo: Lawyer and Mystic*. Philadelphia: Jewish Publication Society.

Wheeler, M. A., D. T. Stuss, and E. Tulving. 1997. "Toward a theory of episodic memory: the frontal lobes and autonoetic consciousness." *Psychol Bull* 121 (3):331–54.

Williams, D. 1956. "The structure of emotions reflected in epileptic experiences." *Brain* 79 (1):29–67.

Wilson, M. 2002. "Six views of embodied cognition." *Psychon Bull Rev* 9 (4):625–36.

Wilson, S. M., A. P. Saygin, M. I. Sereno, and M. Iacoboni. 2004. "Listening to speech activates motor areas involved in speech production." *Nat Neurosci* 7 (7):701–2.

Wirszubski, H. 1969. "Liber Redemptionis: an early version of Kabbalistic commentary to the Guide for the Perplexed of Abraham Abulafia in the Latin translation of Flavius Mythridates." *Proceedings of the Israeli National Academy of Sciences* 3:135–49.

Wolfson, E. R. 1994. *Through a Speculum That Shines: Vision and Imagination in Medieval Jewish Mysticism*. Princeton, NJ: Princeton University Press.

———. 1993. "Forms of visionary ascent as ecstatic experience in the Zoharic literature." In *Gershom Scholem's Major Trends in Jewish Mysticism, 50 years*, edited by P. Schaefer and J. Dan, 209–35. Tubingen: Mohr.

———. 2000. *Abraham Abulafia—Kabbalist and Prophet: Hermeneutics, Theosophy, and Theurgy*. Los Angeles: Cherub.

Wolfson, H. A. 1968. *Philo*. Cambridge: Harvard University Press.

Womelsdorf, T., J. M. Schoffelen, R. Oostenveld, W. Singer, R. Desimone, A. K. Engel, and P. Fries. 2007. "Modulation of neuronal interactions through neuronal synchronization." *Science* 316:1609–12.

Xu, B., J. Grafman, W. D. Gaillard, K. Ishii, F. Vega-Bermudez, P. Pietrini, P. Reeves-Tyer, P. DiCamillo, and W. Theodore. 2001. "Conjoint and extended neural networks for the computation of speech codes: the neural basis of selective impairment in reading words and pseudo-words." *Cereb Cortex* 11 (3):267–77.

Yeo, B. T, F. M. Krienen, J. Sepulcre, M. R. Sabuncu, et al. 2011. "The organization of the human cerebral cortex estimated by intrinsic functional connectivity." *J Neurophysiol* 106:1125–65.

Zacks, J., B. Rypma, J. D. Gabrieli, B. Tversky, and G. H. Glover. 1999. "Imagined transformations of bodies: an fMRI investigation." *Neuropsychologia* 37 (9):1029–40.

Zaehner, R. 1958. *At Sundry Times: An Essay in the Comparison of Religions.* London: Faber and Faber.

Zamboni, G., C. Budriesi, and P. Nichelli. 2005. " 'Seeing oneself': a case of autoscopy." *Neurocase* 11 (3):212–15.

Zimmer, H. 1960. "On the significance of the Indian tantric yoga." In *Spiritual Disciplines*, edited by J. Campbell, 58. Princeton, NJ: Princeton University Press.

Acknowledgments

The encounter of Kabbalistic material with altered perceptions and conscious states in healthy people and neurological patients was the result of the meeting of the authors with Professor Olaf Blanke, director of the Laboratory of Cognitive Neuroscience and the Center for Neuroprosthetics, Bertarelli Foundation Chair in Cognitive Neuroprosthetics, at the Swiss Federal Institute of Technology (EPFL), Lausanne, and Professor Theodor Landis, head of the Department of Neurology at Geneva University Hospital. Together with Professor Peter Brugger from the University Hospital in Zurich, they were among the first to scientifically investigate the phenomenology and underlying neurological mechanism of autoscopic phenomena. This encounter gave rise to a paper in the *Journal of Consciousness Studies* (Arzy, Idel, Landis, and Blanke, "Speaking with One's Self," which partially makes up chapter 3 in this book), and we are grateful to our co-authors as well as to the editors of this journal, especially the Reverend Doctor Anthony Freeman. The fourfold characterization of ecstatic experiences was first presented at the Eranos conference in Ascona in August 2004 and published later (Idel, "On the Language of Ecstatic Experiences in Jewish Mysticism").

Many friends and colleagues have contributed much to the creation and improvement of this book. Professors Tamir Ben-Hur and Oded Abramsky, heads of the Neurology Department at Hadassah Hebrew University Medical Center, greatly encouraged the efforts in writing this book through fruitful and rich discussions. Professor Steven C. Schachter of Harvard Medical School has read the entire book, and besides important comments, also contributed a thoughtful foreword. Didi and Yona Arzi and Tami Ben-David helped to keep the work in line during thoughtful and forbearing discussions. Professors Peter Brugger (University Hospital Zurich), Mordechai Rotenberg (Hebrew University), and Howard L. Weiner (Harvard Medical School) read a preliminary version of the manuscript, and we are grateful to them for this as well. Doctor Istvan Molnar-Szakacs from the Semel Institute for Neuroscience and Human Behavior, University of California Los Angeles, kindly edited Appendix A. Doctor Mark Berman from the Hebrew University in Jerusalem proofread chapter 4. Mr. Francis Ben-Meir and the late Mme. Beatrice Meyer helped greatly in the Jerusalem-Geneva collaboration. The community of scholars at the Hebrew University of Jerusalem and the Hadassah Medical Center is an inexhaustible intellectual source. In particular, Professors Yehuda Liebes, Hermona Soreq, Shoshi Altuvia, Amir Amedi, Yonatan Loewenstein and Hagai Bergman enrich us permanently with their deep insights into scientific creativity. The interface between natural science and the humanities was much supported by Professor Sorin Solomon of the Racah Institute of Physics. Mor Nitzan, also of the Racah Institute contributed important insights to topics discussed in this book and to ongoing scientific work and ideas. Short extracts from this book were published in the Hebrew and English editions of the daily newspaper *Haaretz*, and we thank Benny Ziffer and the editors of *Haaretz* for presenting this work to the interested public. These as usual profited from the eternally helpful eyes of our Hebrew editor, Tirtsah Arzi. The work on this book was supported by the Templeton Foundation within the framework of the Immortality Project, led by Professor John M Fischer; the Yeshaya Horowitz Association, through the Centre of Complexity Science (CCS); the HUJI-EPFL collaboration, and the Marie Curie Intra-European Fellowship, within the framework of the EU-FP7. Our colleagues in the Neuropsychiatry Lab at the Hadassah Hebrew University Medical School—Michael Peer, Noam Saadon-Grosman, Roey Schurr, Inbar Naor, Greg Founshtein, Racheli Fried, and Lakach Yanao—with the continuous help of Yochai Levi and Ronen Shilo, use their unique talents to create new exciting works for better understanding of the human self and its breakdown in neuropsychiatric conditions.

The publication of a book is a long and complicated process. Mrs. Elisabetta Zevi was most influential in the reshaping of the original manuscript into its current, and we hope comprehensive and coherent, form. Mrs. Susanna Zevi, Mrs. Francesca Comboni, and Mr. Glen Hartley are also responsible for making this manuscript into a book. Special thanks to Doctor Laura Major and Jessie Dolch and Susan Laity, the book's editors, for paying special attention to details and giving important suggestions. Heather Gold helped much in advancing the book through editing and production. Mrs. Haya Cohen generously allowed her precious artwork to be used to illustrate the jacket. Finally and most important we are grateful to Jennifer Banks, Executive Editor at Yale University Press, for her help and encouragement through the process of bringing this book to print.

Index

lesions, 127; subconscious
activation of distributed
networks, 136; top-down control
originating in, 135–36, 137
premotor cortex, 108
primary auditory cortex, 122fig.8
primary sensorimotor cortices,
122fig.8
principium individuationis, 15
procedural memory, 104, 105,
108, 125
prophecy: in Abulafia's ecstatic
experiences, 42, 46–47, 143;
ecstatic experiences and, 22,
27–28, 46–47, 55–56, 58, 143;
medieval views of, 28; on
messianism of Sabbatai Zevi, 97;
trembling to obtain, 46;
unio-mystica and, 24–25
prophetic Kabbalah, 2, 42, 62–63,
142, 145
prosody and intonation, 125
psychoanalytical approach to
mystical experiences, 6, 7
PTSD. *See* posttraumatic stress
disorder

Qalqish, Elnathan ben-Moshe,
60–61, 72, 73, 74

rapture, 22, 23
Recanati, Menahem, 51–52
recitation of texts, 49, 91, 92–93, 94,
95–98, 100, 102t.2
religion, mysticism as key to, 24–26
rest, default-mode network activity
during, 132
Reuchlin, Johannes, 145
right hemisphere, 80, 122fig.8,
125, 131

right-left judgments, 45fig.2c
right posterior parietal cortex,
128–29
right TPJ, 78, 79fig.3, 80

Sabbatai Zevi (Sabbateanism), 2,
24, 97–98, 99
Sabbateanism (Sabbatai Zevi), 2,
24, 97–98, 99
Safedian Kabbalah, 47, 48–49, 91,
144. *See also* Lurianic Kabbalah;
Vital, Hayim
saint veneration, 95–96
Samson of Ostropol, 91
Scholem, Gershom, 22–24, 26,
28, 145
Sefer 'Avodath ha-Qodesh
(Ibn-Gabbai), 58
Sefer 'Avodath Yisra'el (Maggid of
Kuznitz), 92–93
Sefer ha-Hayim, 62–63, 72, 73
Sefer ha-Hesheq (Abulafia), 46,
53, 54
Sefer ha-Hezionoth (Vital), 63,
95–96
Sefer ha-Meshiv, 91
Sefer ha-Oth (Abulafia), 53–54
Sefer ha-Tamar, 91
Sefer ha-Tzeruf, 51
Sefer Hayei Haolam Haba
(Abulafia), 53
Sefer Yetzirah, 143
sefirotic Kabbalah, 11, 142, 145
self: alteration of sense of, 31;
asomatognosia, 32; in cognitive
neuroscience, 2, 32–34; corporeal
awareness of, 36, 37fig.1, 41, 59,
68–69, 123, 124fig.9; disruption
of spatial unity with body, 33;
dramatic shifts in, 31–32;